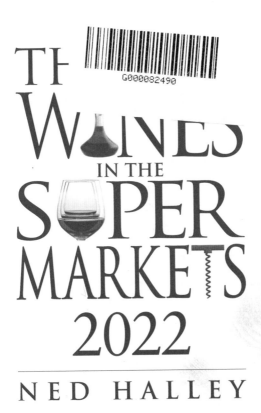

THE WINES IN THE SUPER MARKETS 2022

NED HALLEY

foulsham
LONDON • NEW YORK • TORONTO • SYDNEY

W. Foulsham & Co. Ltd

for Foulsham Publishing Ltd

The Old Barrel Store, Drayman's Lane, Marlow, Bucks SL7 2FF

Foulsham books can be found in all good bookshops and direct from www.foulsham.com

ISBN: 978-0-572-04816-7

Text copyright © 2021 Ned Halley
Series, format and layout design © 2021 Foulsham Publishing

Cover photographs © Thinkstock

A CIP record for this book is available from the British Library

The moral right of the author has been asserted

Printed and bound in Great Britain by Martins the Printers Ltd

Contents

—*Another vintage year*—

Detect an air of resignation in the headline above? In the second year of Covid-19 any intimation of irony is surely allowable. It's difficult even for a moment to feel immune to the sheer weariness, let alone fear and dread, of the consequences of the perpetual pandemic.

But this is an annual book about wine, so every year is a vintage year. You could say the constant renewal, grape harvest after grape harvest, is reassuring. And the end product is definitely a potential source of comfort. So, welcome to *The Best Wines in the Supermarkets 2022*. Undaunted, unbowed, brimming with hope for all the vintages to come, your guide is before you once again.

It hasn't been any easier to compose these pages this year than last. The generous wine tastings that have long been staged annually for media hacks like me by the leading retailers simply ceased as Covid struck (or was acknowledged to have struck) in March 2020. I have not attended any such tastings since.

So I have been shopping. In a well-planned campaign since the early summer of 2021 I have cruised the aisles of countless supermarkets clutching carefully constructed lists of the wines I need to try and swooping when they are on offer at their very keenest promotional prices. It has cost a lot, but by buying at discounts sometimes close to 50 per cent, I've been able to compile notes, most of them enthusiastic, on about 300 individual wines.

I have been asked, why don't you ask the supermarkets to send you free samples? I answer: because I won't. Most would not even entertain the idea anyway. I am not a celebrity wine writer (but did you see me on Channel 4's brilliant *Sunday Brunch* programme? I've been on a few times in the last year) and I am not just a wine writer either. I'm a bloody-minded journalist with a certain independence of mind to live up to.

Apologies for talking about me. It has not been my custom, and it stops here. Time to review the market.

There have been lots of price drops. Yes, in spite of Brexit, rising inflation and the fearsome complications of making and shipping wine in the midst of a worldwide outbreak of a deadly disease. Many list prices have reduced, and discounting is rife.

It is, of course, market forces. Global demand for wine dwindled dramatically in 2020–21. In Britain, the lengthy periods of closure for what we must now call the 'hospitality industry' have diminished or deleted a huge section of the wine market. Reports that the 'off' trade – high street and online merchants as well as supermarkets – have taken up all the slack are misplaced. Take-home sales of alcohol during lockdowns might have increased, but much more for beer and spirits than wine. And given that 'on' sales (in pubs, restaurants etc) have long accounted for nearly half of all alcohol sales, overall consumption has fallen steeply.

If there's an upside, it's that wine drinkers have been trading up. Industry figures show that during the pandemic period, sales of sub-£5 wines have declined by about 40 per cent. Wines priced between £5 and £7 now account for 53 per cent of the total and those between £7 and £9 have increased in market share from 8 to 11 per cent.

Of course this might merely mean we're paying more for the same wines. But there's apparently no evidence for that, in England anyway (see Devolved Wine Pricing box). And excise duty, which does as much to adjust the price of cheaper wines as anything else, was once again frozen in the 2021 Budget – the second successive year in which blessed Chancellor Rishi Sunak (a teetotaller) has extended this most unusual concession.

The supermarkets continue to use discounting as their principal instrument of wine-sales promotion, and in this year's guide I'm anxious to remind hard-pressed readers of this almost universal benevolence. The Big Four chains: Asda, Morrisons, Sainsbury's and Tesco, now all regularly feature 25% off any six or more bottle deals. Look out for these not just at Easter and Christmas but over bank holidays and half-terms. Even Waitrose occasionally follows suit, in between its perpetual promotions on scores of individual wines. Co-op offers are sketchier, and Marks & Spencer too (they seem to have abandoned the 25%-off case purchases that were a regular feature online).

Oddly enough, the only leading retailers not employing any significant pattern of discounting on their wines are the Teutonic twins Aldi and Lidl, now familiarly known as The Discounters. I guess when you're already a discounter it rather gives the game away when you start offering discounts on your discounts.

This is a personal view, but I don't believe for a minute that the wines of either of these outfits, both of which I liked a lot better when they were cheerfully known as 'no-frills supermarkets' are in any meaningful way better or better value than their rivals. There, I've said it.

And so to the wider world of wine. How are things out in the vineyards of Europe and beyond? They can't be all that bad, because even in the pandemic years of 2020 and 2021 production of wine has continued. 2020 wasn't a bad one for winemakers in either hemisphere. Climate conditions were reasonably kind and harvests have not been significantly diminished by Covid-19. It's true that European harvests in 2021 have been widely and sometimes seriously diminished by late frosts. But dramatic shortfalls in production are myth. Southern hemisphere producers, who harvest mostly in March–April (as opposed to September–October in the north) have reported benevolent conditions and satisfactory volumes.

There continues to be an excess of supply in the wine world. There's no pressure on prices from that direction. If there is a negative force in the market, it's the old one: The Evils of Drink. The social engineers of the anti-alcohol lobby, as I see them, have found a new platform in this wretched hour of pandemic, perfectly embodied in the words of the World Health Organisation on its website. Those concerned for their well-being who might seek consolation in a glass of wine are instructed: 'Avoid alcohol altogether', on the grounds that it might 'undermine your own immune system'.

That this is nonsense is beyond doubt. But the question remains: why do publicly funded bodies persist in making pronouncements such as this?

Something quietly to contemplate in the company of a glass of good wine.

Devolved Wine Pricing

The House of Commons 2020 briefing paper entitled *Alcohol: minimum pricing* starts with this summary: 'The debate about a minimum price for alcohol has been prompted by concerns about high levels of drinking, its effect on public health and public order, and a widespread belief that most of the alcohol that contributes to drunken behaviour is irresponsibly priced and sold'.

In short, it's those who sell alcohol who are to blame. The answer in England is to prevent the sale of intoxicating drinks below a 'permitted price' – defined as the excise duty and VAT on the duty on the drink in question, under a 2014 amendment to the Licensing Act of 2003. So, in England, you can't sell a 75cl bottle of table wine for under £2.68.

In Scotland and Wales, the excise duty and VAT is the same as in England. But alcohol policy is devolved. The respective intranational governments have decided that the UK overall pricing policy is insufficient. In 2018, Scotland introduced minimum retail pricing based on 50 pence per unit of alcohol. In 2020, Wales followed suit.

The purpose is to discourage the sales of cheap, high-alcohol products such as white cider and extra-strength beers as well as cut-price spirits. But the cheapest table wines are affected too. A 75cl bottle of 12% abv delivers 9 units of alcohol so cannot be priced below £4.50 – and so on. At Aldi, as an example, about 20 wines are affected, and the company will not sell any of them in Scotland and Wales, or allow orders for home delivery to addresses in those countries.

Is it working? Initial research is pointing to lower alcohol consumption in 'problem' households. There are no plans to introduce this measure in England, but Westminster is maintaining a watching brief.

Where does the best wine come from?

It's France, I suppose. Fabled estates in Bordeaux, Burgundy and Champagne have a perpetual monopoly on the most-venerated red, white and sparkling wines, worldwide. If your budget per bottle starts at £100 I guess that's all you need to know. But for those of us who buy wine in supermarkets and consider even £10 a bit of a punt, the question needs to be readdressed.

In the global context, you could argue that the country of origin of any wine is immaterial. But the supermarkets wouldn't agree with you. They arrange all the wines in their stores and on their websites precisely according to their nationality.

It's quite odd. You wouldn't display your canned fruits and vegetables this way, would you? Or your frozen fish? Or anything else, really? But that's the way they do the wine and, accordingly, that's the way I arrange the listings in this book.

To be fair, the wines of particular nations and regions do have identifiable attributes even when made from a common grape variety. The white wines from fashionable Sauvignon Blanc, for example, have distinct styles at home in France's Loire Valley and away in the Marlborough region of New Zealand. Chilean Sauvignon has its own qualities, and so does South African.

Germany, though never in fashion, makes inimitably delicious wines from the Riesling grape. Australian wines from this noble variety are so different that I suspect uninitiated devotees of the Mosel and Rhine would hardly recognise a Clare Valley Riesling at all.

While the grape does much to determine the nature of the wine, location still counts for a lot. Landscape and soil conditions, weather and the peculiar skills and customs of the winemakers all have their parts to play.

The French have a word for it: *terroir*, which loosely translates as 'soil', but *vignerons* in France take it to mean the entirety of conditions local to the site of crop production. That's not just the soil but the lie of the land, its geographical position, its climate and indeed what the tillers of that soil and the custodians of the crops get up to.

On visits to France, I have heard much of terroir. Amid the most-valued vineyards of Chablis I have learned that the ground is composed largely of oyster shells, mountainised over millennia into vertiginous slopes. From these bleak, frost-ravaged heights come some of the world's most minerally luscious dry white wines. I've had it all endlessly explained to me and never really understood, but be in no doubt: *grand cru* Chablis is like no other wine.

And so on across all of France. Elsewhere, winemakers might not speak of terroir, but they all believe in the real or imagined unique properties of their estates. They all consider their wines to be an expression of their locations and traditions. This is what gives wine its much-treasured diversity, and of course its mystique. Wine is more than a mere nutritious drug. It's part natural phenomenon, part art form. Hurrah to that, I say.

It's all about the
grape variety

The grape, naturally, counts for everything in wine. The finished product is, after all, simply the fermented juice of the fruit. Well, yes, there will be a cultured yeast introduced to assist the process. And there are permitted additives, mostly sulphur products and clarifying agents, to ensure healthy, bright wine. The wine's natural sugars and acids can be supplemented.

But the grape variety still sets the pace. Dark-skinned grapes make red wine because the skins are included in the must (pressed juice) during fermentation and give the wine its colour. The juice of virtually all grapes is clear. You can make white wine with dark-skinned grapes by extracting the juice promptly and fermenting it free of the skins. The base wine for Champagne is made largely from dark-skinned grapes. But still white wine is made much more simply – from pale-skinned grapes fermented without their skins.

Different grape varieties produce correspondingly different wines. There are hundreds of distinct varieties, but a couple of dozen account for most production. All of us have favourites, or at least preferences. The varieties described here account for most of the wines on offer in the supermarkets.

Red wine varieties

Aglianico: Ancient variety of southern Italy said to have been imported by immigrant Greek farmers around 500 BC. The name is a recent rendering of former Ellenico ('Hellenic') and the grape has caught on again thanks to Aglianico del Vulture, a volcanic DOC of Basilicata. The wines are dark, intense, pungent and long-lived.

Barbera: The most widely planted dark-skinned grape of Piedmont in northwest Italy makes easy-drinking purple vigorous rasping red wine to enjoy young and also, increasingly, a darker, denser but still vigorous style given gravitas through oak-ageing. Mostly sold under denominations Barbera d'Asti and Barbera d'Alba. Unrelated to Barbaresco, a Piedmontese wine made from Nebbiolo grapes.

Cabernet Sauvignon: Originally of Bordeaux and the mainstay of claret, Cabernet berries are compact and thick-skinned, making wine of intense flavour and gripping tannin. The grandest wines need decades to develop their full bloom. Everyday wines made worldwide typically have dense colour, purple in youth, aromas of blackcurrants and cedar wood ('cigar box') and firm, juicy-savoury fruit.

Gamay: It's the grape of Beaujolais. Colour can be purple with a blue note; nose evokes new-squashed raspberries with perhaps a pear drop or two, the effect of carbonic maceration, the Beaujolais method of vinification. Fruit flavours are juicy, bouncing, even refreshing.

Grenache: The French name for the Garnacha, originally of Spain, where it is much employed in Rioja and other classic regions. HQ in France is the southern Rhône Valley with further widespread plantings across the country's Mediterranean regions. Wines can be light in colour but emphatic in flavour with a wild, hedgerow-fruit style lifted with spice and pepper. Widely cultivated across the New World.

Malbec: The signature grape of Argentina. A native of Bordeaux, where it plays a minor blending role, it thrives in the high-altitude vineyards of Mendoza, a province of the Andean foothills. The best wines have dark colour and a perfume sometimes fancifully said to evoke leather and liquorice; flavours embrace briary black fruits with suggestions of bitter chocolate, plum and spice.

Merlot: Bordeaux variety very often partnering Cabernet Sauvignon in claret blends and also solo in fabled Pomerol wines including Château Petrus. The grape is large and thin-skinned compared to Cabernet, making wine of rich ruby colour with scents evoking black cherry and cassis and fruit that can be round and rich. Ordinary wines are soft, mellow and early developing but might lack the firmness of tannin that gives balance.

Pinot Noir: It's the solo grape of red burgundy and one of three varieties in champagne. Everyday Pinot wines typically have a bright, translucent ruby colour and aromas evoking red soft summer fruits and cherries. Flavours correspond. Fine Pinot has elegant weight and shape, mysteriously alluring. New Zealand makes distinctive, delicious, sinewy Pinots; Chile produces robust and earthy Pinots; California's best Pinots compare for quality with fabulously expensive Burgundies.

Sangiovese: The grape of Chianti, so-named after the Latin for 'the blood of Jove', makes pleasingly weighted, attractively coloured wines with plummy perfume, even pruny in older wines, and slinky flavours evoking blackcurrant, raspberry and occasionally nectarine. Good Chianti always has a clear tannic edge, giving the wine its trademark nutskin-dry finish.

Syrah: At home in southern France, the Syrah makes wines that at their best are densely coloured, rich in aromas of sun-baked blackberries, silky in texture and plumply, darkly, spicily flavoured. The grandest pure-Syrah wines, such as Hermitage and Côte Rôtie, are gamey, ripe and rich and very long-lived. Syrah is widely planted across Mediterranean France as a blending grape in wines of the Côtes du Rhône and Languedoc. Under the name Shiraz, Syrah is Australia's most prolific red-wine variety.

Tempranillo: The grape at the heart of Rioja has to work hard. The unique selling point of the region's famous red wines is the long ageing process in oak casks that gives the finished product its creamy, vanilla richness – which can all too easily overwhelm the juiciness and freshness of the wine. The Tempranillo's bold blackcurranty-minty aromas and flavours stand up well to the test, and the grape's thick skin imparts handsome ruby colour that doesn't fade as well as firm tannins that keep the wine in shape even after many years in cask or bottle. Tempranillo is widely planted throughout Spain, and in Portugal, under numerous assumed names.

White wine varieties

Albariño: Rightly revered Iberian variety once better known in its Minho Valley, Portugal, manifestation as Alvarinho, a mainstay of vinho verde wine. Since the 1980s, Albariño from Spain's Galicia region, immediately north of Portugal, has been making aromatic and scintillatingly racy sea-fresh dry white wines from vineyards often planted close to the Atlantic shore. The seaside DO of Rias Baixas, now a major centre for gastro-tourism, is the heart of Albariño country. The variety, characterized by small, thick-skinned berries with many pips, is now also cultivated in California, New Zealand and beyond.

Chardonnay: Universal variety still at its best at home in Burgundy for simple appley fresh dry wines all the way up to lavish new-oak-fermented deluxe appellations such as Meursault and Montrachet making ripe, complex, creamy-nutty and long-developing styles. Imitated in Australia and elsewhere with mixed success.

Chenin Blanc: Loire Valley variety cultivated for dry, sweet and sparkling white wines, some of them among France's finest. Honeyed aromas and zesty acidity equally characterize wines including elegant, mineral AOP Vouvray and opulent, golden late-harvested

AOP Coteaux du Layon. In South Africa, Chenin Blanc now makes many fascinating and affordable wines.

Fiano: Revived southern Italian variety makes dry but nuanced wines of good colour with aromas of orchard fruit, almonds and candied apricots and finely balanced fresh flavours. Fleetingly fashionable and worth seeking out.

Glera: Widely planted in the Veneto region of northeast Italy, it's the principal variety in prosecco sparkling wine. The grape itself used to be named prosecco, after the winemaking village of Prosecco near Treviso, but under a 2009 change to the wine-denomination rules, the name can now be applied exclusively to the wine, not the grape. Glera makes a neutral base wine with plenty of acidity. It is a prolific variety, and needs to be. Sales of prosecco in Britain have now surpassed those of champagne.

Palomino Fino: The grape that makes sherry. The vines prosper in the *albariza*, the sandy, sun-bleached soil of Andalucia's Jerez region, providing a pale, bone-dry base wine ideally suited to the sherry process. All proper sherry of every hue is white wine from Palomino Fino. The region's other grape, the Pedro Ximenez, is used as a sweetening agent and to make esoteric sweet wines.

Pinot Grigio: At home in northeast Italy, it makes dry white wines of pale colour and frequently pale flavour too. The mass-market wines' popularity might owe much to their natural low acidity. The better wines are aromatic, fleetingly smoky and satisfyingly weighty in the manner of Pinot Gris made in the French province of Alsace. New Zealand Pinot Gris or Pinot Grigio follows the Alsace style.

Riesling: Native to Germany, it makes unique wines pale in colour with sharp-apple aromas and racy, sleek fruit whether dry or sweet according to labyrinthine local winemaking protocols. Top-quality Rhine and Mosel Rieslings age wonderfully, taking on golden hues and a fascinating 'petrolly' resonance. Antipodean Rieslings have more colour and weight often with a mineral, limey twang.

Sauvignon Blanc: Currently fashionable thanks to New Zealand's inspired adoption of the variety for assertive, peapod-nettle-seagrass styles. Indigenous Sauvignons from France's Loire Valley have rapidly caught up, making searingly fresh wines at all levels from generic Touraine up to high-fallutin' Sancerre. Delicate, elegant Bordeaux Sauvignon is currently on top form too.

Semillon: Along with Sauvignon Blanc, a key component of white Bordeaux, including late-harvested, golden sweet wines such as Sauternes. Even in dry wines, colour ranges up to rich yellow, aromas evoke tropical fruits and honeysuckle, exotic flavours lifted by citrus presence. Top Australian Semillons rank among the world's best.

Viognier: Formerly fashionable but perpetually interesting variety of the Rhône Valley makes white wines of pleasing colour with typical apricot aroma and almondy-orchardy fruit; styles from quite dry to fruitily plump.

More about these varieties and many others in 'A wine vocabulary' starting on page 158.

Brand awareness

Big-brand wines such as Blossom Hill and Hardy do not crowd the pages of this book. I do get to taste them, and leave most of them out. I believe they don't measure up for quality, interest or value.

The best wines in the supermarkets are very often own-brands. Own-brands date back to the 1970s, when interest in wine finally began to take root in Britain. Sainsbury's was first, with its own Claret, about 1975. It was hardly a revolutionary idea. Grand merchants like Berry Bros & Rudd (est 1698) had been doing own-label Bordeaux and much else besides, for ever.

In the supermarket sector, wine was bought on the wholesale market like anything else, from butter to washing powder. Only when interest in wine started to extend beyond the coterie served by the merchants did the mass retailers take any notice. It was thanks, of course, to the new craze for foreign travel, and to the good influence of writers like Elizabeth David, who revealed the joys of Continental-style food and drink. In 1966, Hugh Johnson's brilliant and accessible book *Wine* piqued the public consciousness as never before.

The adoption of supermarket wine was slow enough, but accelerated in the 1980s by the arrival of new, decent wines from Australia. Earlier on, cheap Aussie wines had been overripe, stewed rubbish, but breakthrough technology now enabled fresh, bold reds and whites of a different stripe. Wretched Europlonk brands like Hirondelle retreated before a tide of lush Chardonnay and 'upfront' Shiraz.

The horizon for supermarket wine buyers, always shackled by price constraint, was suddenly widened. In spite of the delivery distances, southern hemisphere producers could match their Old World counterparts for value as well as interest and quality.

In time, the winemakers of Europe fought back. Top estates carried on with 'fine wine' production, but humbler enterprises had to learn how to master real quality at the everyday level. They did. I believe the huge improvements in the simpler wines of the Continent owe much to the need to match the competition from the New World.

By the 1990s, Britain had become the world's biggest wine importer. Supermarkets were largely responsible, and now had muscle in the market. They started to dispatch their own people to vineyards and wineries worldwide, not just to buy the wines but to participate in their production. And always, they demanded the lowest-possible prices.

And so to today's proliferation of supermarket own-brands. They are the flagships of every one of the big grocers, and usually the focal point of promotions. They are, naturally enough, the wines of which their begetters are most proud. Mass-market brands do still persist in the supermarkets. Some are very good. I think of Blason, Chasse and Vieille Ferme from France; Baron de Ley and Miguel Torres from Spain; McGuigan and Penfolds from Australia; Catena from Argentina and Concha y Toro from Chile, among others.

If you have a favourite popular brand, do check the index to this book on page 187. It might not be mentioned in the entry for the supermarket where you're used to finding it, but that doesn't mean I've left it out.

Pick of the year

I have awarded maximum points to 35 wines this year – more than usual out of a smaller overall total than usual. I put this down to sentimental enthusiasm in these troubled times for us all, but the sentiment is nonetheless sincere.

In this entirely personal selection, I discover that among the producing nations, first place goes to France with 15 top-scoring wines, nearly half the total. Does this signify anything beyond my own individual preferences or loyalties? Probably not. But I can't help myself.

Runner-up is, unsurprisingly, Italy on 7. What does surprise me, though, is that Italy should be that far behind the leader. Looking back, I seem to recall more outstanding Italian wines than anything else. I suspect there are more Italian wines in these pages than any other.

Spain follows up with 5 and Germany on 3. Australia scores 2 and there's 1 apiece to England, New Zealand and Portugal.

In the league of retailers, few surprises. Waitrose comes first with 9 top buys. Tesco is next with 6, then the Co-op and Sainsbury's both with 5, Majestic on 4 and 2 apiece to Asda, Aldi and Morrisons. Zilch for Lidl or Marks & Spencer. What can you do?

Red wines

Grignan-les-Aldhémar 2019	Asda	£6.00
The guv'nor	Majestic	£6.99
Palladino Biferno Rosso Riserva 2017	Co-op	£7.00
Vanita Puglia Negroamaro 2019	Co-op	£7.30
Loron Beaujolais 2020	Majestic	£7.99
Domaine des Ormes Saumur 2018	Co-op	£8.00
Salice Salentino Borgodei Trulli 2019	Waitrose	£8.99
The Voyage Durif 2019	Aldi	£8.99
Ara Select Blocks Pinot Noir 2020	Sainsbury's	£9.00
M Chapoutier Côtes du Rhône Villages 2019	Tesco	£9.00
Saumur Les Nivières 2018	Waitrose	£9.99
Terre di Faiano Primitivo 2020	Waitrose	£9.99
Taste the Difference Pic St Loup 2018	Sainsbury's	£10.00
Cantina del Nebb Nebbiolo 2018	Waitrose	£12.99
Wirra Wirra Church Block 2018	Waitrose	£13.49

White wines

Riesling QbA Rheinhessen 2019	Sainsbury's	£5.25
Cuvée Pêcheur 2020	Waitrose	£5.49
Finest St Mont 2019	Tesco	£6.50
Dr L Riesling 2019	Asda	£7.00
Vanita Grillo 2020	Co-op	£7.00
Vouvray La Couronne des Plantagenets 2019	Sainsbury's	£7.25
Minea Greco di Tufa 2018	Morrisons	£8.75
Definition Sauternes 2010	Majestic	£9.99
Guigal Côtes du Rhône 2018	Tesco	£12.00
The Best Marques de Los Rios Rioja Reserva 2016	Morrisons	£13.00
Dr Hermann Ürziger Würzgarten Riesling Auslese 2005	Majestic	£14.99

Sparkling wines

Crémant de Jura 2018	Aldi	£8.49
Cave de Lugny Crémant de Bourgogne Blanc de Blancs	Waitrose	£13.49
Balfour 1503 Foxwood Cuvee	Co-op	£17.00
Finest Premier Cru Champagne Brut	Tesco	£20.00

Sainsbury's Blanc de Noirs Champagne Brut	Sainsbury's	£21.00

Fortified wines

Finest Fino Sherry	Tesco	£6.00
Waitrose Amontillado Medium Dry Sherry	Waitrose	£7.69
Cayetano del Pino Y Cia Palo Cortado Solera Sherry	Waitrose	£10.99
Finest 10-Year-Old Tawny Port	Tesco	£12.00

Aldi

None of my nearest branches of Aldi seems to stock more than a minimal choice from the award-winning wine range (Multiple Drinks Retailer of the Year 2020), so I had to resort to extremes. I went online.

I did not have to do this in 2020, as Aldi managed to be the only supermarket chain to stage its spring wine tasting for the media before the March lockdown. And in fairness in 2021 Aldi was the first of the retailers to put on a tasting in 2021 – but sadly, it was too late in the year for me: past my lead time for this book.

So, in the summer I ordered lots of wines for a tasting of my own. I'm glad to say it all went remarkably well. I could cope with the website and went for wines I was reasonably confident would be worth trying. My wines were duly and promptly delivered at a charge of £4.95. Thirty or so of my selection, I'm glad to say, have made the cut. They are all under £10 except the two very decent champagnes, and there are plenty of wines entirely new to me at Aldi, including a fine holiday dry white from Greece and a really memorable red from Uruguay made from the world's healthiest grape variety.

One in four of all the wines comes from Italy. This might betray my own instinctive preferences – it was me who chose the tasting line-up after all – but I like to think Aldi is showing some expertise in this corner of the wine world. I'm also pleased to report that two good German wines have made it in this year. More, please, Aldi, in light of your nation of origin.

Although I find Aldi stores as bewildering as ever in their layout and stock unreliability, the wine range seems to me to be showing material improvement in its scope and presentation. I'm happy that the over-elaborated 'Exquisite Collection' range description has been dropped, and while the seemingly random French-wine branding Pierre Jaurant and Italian Castellore persist, I can live with them when the wines are as good as those I've tried.

And the wines genuinely are good. I know it's the prices that are supposed to give Aldi the edge, but I don't believe the range is actually all that much cheaper than big rivals like Asda, Morrisons and Tesco, especially in this time of mass discounting. Aldi and Lidl might be collectively known as The Discounters, but neither does 25% off the whole range in the way the giant multiples do.

The main attraction of Aldi wine as far as I can see is the steadily improving quality and diversity of the range. Which is just fine with me.

RED WINES

8 Buenas Vides Malbec 2020   £5.79

This 'Specially Selected' Uco Valley (high altitude) juicy midweight wine has blackberry vigour and an authentic Malbec frame of fruit flavours; 14% alcohol.

8 Buenas Vides Criolla Grande 2020   £5.99

Criolla Grande, a black-skinned grape variety cultivated in Argentina's Mendoza region, has so far mostly gone into cheap bulk wines – white, pink or red – but is now manifesting under its own name. If you like lightweight bright cherry-raspberry reds, do try this one; 13.5% alcohol.

9 Cocodrilo Malbec 2019   £9.99

Smart-looking all-black package from a well-known Mendoza estate, Vinas Cobos, is among Aldi's 'Classic Icons' range and available only online. It's classic indeed, darkly ripe, big with blackberry-spicy aromas, velvet-cushiony in texture, and richly savoury, prompting imaginings of buffed soft leather, bitter chocolate and sweet raisins; 14% alcohol.

10 The Voyage Durif 2020   £8.99

Well who saw this coming? It's from Aldi's 'Classic Icons' range and therefore available only online, but in spite of that I'm top-scoring it because it is a genuinely delectable Aussie wine of untypical style and sensibly priced. The Durif vine, originally (1880s) of southern France and now unknown there has lately prospered in Australia's Victoria State and makes robust, dark and pruny bold reds of which this is a very amenable example. I liked its blackberry-pie generosity, rustic spice and nifty tannic clean finish, and I liked its style; 13.5% alcohol.

ARGENTINA

AUSTRALIA

RED WINES

♆ 9 Specially Selected Rasteau 2019   £8.99
A senior Côtes du Rhône Villages AC from a particularly
healthy vintage in which even big ripe wines like this one
(it's 14.5% alcohol) are typically rounded and balanced
with weight, spice and the juiciest of black-fruit flavours.
This isn't particularly cheap, but the quality leaves you in
no doubt it's value for money.

♆ 8 Aimone Vino Rosso d'Italia   £4.99
Non-vintage generic wine made in Liguria, Italy's
northwestern riviera, probably from Primitivo and maybe
Dolcetto, it's middling in colour and weight with cherry
brightness on the nose and palate, pleasant and balanced;
13.5% alcohol. Italian café wine, I call it. Curious
package in a fancy embossed bottle bearing the legend 'to
cheer a special evening, alone or in good company' with
the number 94 on the neck label, denoting the score (out
of 100 I'd guess) allocated the wine by Italian wine judge
Lucca Maroni. All good innocent fun.

♆ 8 Castellore Primitivo Puglia 2019   £4.99
At this price I wasn't expecting much, but this does
not disappoint. Middling-dense purple colour, shy
brambly aroma and a fully-fledged ripe body of gently
spicy blackberry-juicy impressively smooth-running and
complete wine in the best Primitivo tradition; 13.5%
alcohol. Don't be put off by the strange choice of white
screwcap closure and stark white label.

RED WINES

ITALY

🍷 8 **Dojan Barbera d'Asti 2019** £7.49

Made by racily named Roberto Ferraris, this is a serious wine, presumably limited in quantity as it's available only online, and definitely one to try. Deep colour with promising defined crisp brambly nose and impressively intense bouncy hedgerow-fruit savours with plenty of torque (sorry for that but it's 14.5% alcohol) and long, darkly juicy finish coming up clean and bright. Good price for this quality.

🍷 8 **Castellore Valpolicella**
Ripasso Superiore 2018 £7.99

Why does Aldi persist in using such obviously contrived brand names as 'Castellore' for their perfectly decent generic wines? They should stick to their meaningless if well-intentioned 'Specially Selected' slogan – which also happens to be appended to this wine. But never mind – this is cracking ripasso, tasting authentically of cherry-bright Valpolicella and wholesomely fortified with dried-fruit must to give a raisiny, pleasantly abrasive texture as well as weight. Well-managed grip in tandem with healthy ripeness make it a seriously good match for starchy pasta and risotto; 13.5% alcohol.

NEW ZEALAND

🍷 9 **Pinot Vigilante Pinot Noir 2019** £9.99

The name isn't much of a draw, but the wine is certainly worth looking out for. It's a particularly ripe and full Pinot from the Central Otago with traditional cherry aromas fortified with agreeable blueberry notes, and generous juicy red-fruit flavours lifted by defined acidity; 13.5% alcohol. From the 'Classic Icons' range and only available (annoyingly) online.

RED WINES

PORTUGAL

8 **Animus Red Blend 2018** £4.99

Try not to be deterred by the irrelevant branding: this is a thoroughly decent and typical Portuguese melange of unnamed grapes from unnamed regions but recognisably brooding, savoury, minty and herby in the best national tradition; 13% alcohol.

9 **Animus Douro 2019** £5.49

This is terrifically good for the money, dark and sweet but in the best possible way, with a porty pong and spicy black flavours craftily trimmed with a firm but gentle tannin presence; 13% alcohol. Tastes of its place – the Douro Valley where port wine comes from.

URUGUAY

9 **Specially Selected Criollo Tannat 2019** £6.00

Substantial red-meat matcher from Uruguay's Atlantic-facing Maldonado region lives up to its constituent grape's name for dark colour, moody-savoury fruit and firm tannic grip. Tannat is reportedly the number one variety for conducting health-enhancing resveratrol (antioxidant) into the blood of its drinkers. This smooth and plummy monster (14% alcohol) makes a delicious conveyance.

PINK WINES

ENGLAND

8 **Specially Selected English Rosé 2020** £8.99

Not merely a new vintage of last year's likeable Lyme Bay (Devon) pink but a whole new wine from Surrey. It's a vanishingly pale shade of coral and fleetingly strawberry on the nose from the Pinot Noir that leads the blend, with corresponding fruit. Just short of sweet but not without zing; 11.5% alcohol. It's expensive for what it is, but this is English wine, and I salute Aldi for offering it.

PINK WINES

FRANCE

🍷 9 Specially Selected Ventoux Rosé 2020 £6.99
Aldi has a remarkably extensive range of rosés, almost
all of them new to the list in the last couple of years.
Of those I've tasted this Rhône wine is the standout. The
colour is delicately pale polished copper, the nose fresh,
floral and promising and the fruit berry-bright and crisply
refreshing; it's very dry but by no means austere; a rarely
interesting pink in an attractive pot-shaped clear bottle;
13% alcohol.

ROMANIA

🍷 8 Dealuri Rosé 2020 £4.99
Pale coral colour, red-fruit aroma and a corresponding
raspberry savour in this friendly, soft but clean-finishing
aperitif pink; 12% alcohol. Sensible price.

SPAIN

**🍷 8 Specially Selected Baron Amarillo
Rioja Rosado 2020** £6.99
Previous vintages of this have left me cold but I liked this
one for its party-frock colour, whiff of strawberry and
generous plump fruit, lifted by bright acidity. It doesn't
resemble red Rioja, but has a positive charm of its own;
13% alcohol.

WHITE WINES

CHILE

🍷 8 Estevez Viognier 2020 £5.49
This generously ripe dry wine has signature Viognier
apricot notes amid the lush exotic fruits, all in tidy
balance; 13.5% alcohol.

WHITE WINES

FRANCE

🍷 **8** **Pierre Jaurant Sauvignon Blanc** £4.49
I believe this is the same wine previously known as Vignobles Roussellet SB because it has a familiar and likeable tangy, sherbet-gooseberry zest and grassy raciness and a modest 11.5% alcohol. Like its nominal predecessor it is non-vintage but daisy fresh just the same and jolly cheap.

🍷 **9** **Pierre Jaurant Alsace Pinot Blanc 2019** £6.49
This one's out of the blue. Alsace Pinot Blanc is one of France's most distinctive (and least exported) wine styles and you get a good introduction here, especially at the price. Eager orchardy-nutty nose and matching high-toned flavour with a suggestion of blanched-almond creaminess to the racy aromatic fruit; 12.5% alcohol.

GERMANY

🍷 **8** **Blütengarten Riesling 2020** £4.49
Nice dry apple-fresh Rheinhessen QbA aperitif with easy zing and a little residual sugar, pleasant and delicate with Riesling character; 11.5% alcohol.

🍷 **9** **Piesporter Goldtröpfchen Riesling Spätlese 2018** £6.99
Rare treat from Aldi's 'Classic Icons' range which appears to include only one German wine, in spite of Aldi's evident Teutonic origins. Anyway, mustn't moan: this is a delightful sweet-apple aperitif moselle with perfect prickly freshness and lemon tang in balance; a simple formula maybe but one of the finest and least-appreciated wine styles in all the world, at a sensible price; just 9% alcohol. The bad news is that it's only on sale online.

WHITE WINES

GREECE

9 **Filos Estate Assyrtiko 2020** £6.99
Fine mineral dry wine is a blend of Greece's own
Assyrtiko grape with Sauvignon Blanc to make a style
that is certainly Greek: resiny, spicy, tasting as you might
imagine a white wine from vines in a parched, rocky
landscape would be, rather than the fresh fields of France,
say. I like this for its ethnicity as well as its fresh, lemony
Aegean pizzazz; 13% alcohol.

ITALY

8 **Castellore Fiano 2020** £4.99
The Fiano grape of southern Italy was counted as an
ancient Roman legacy when it was revived in the 1990s
but has since been rather left behind by cooler varieties
like Cataratto and Vermentino. Here's a delicately
aromatic dry example from Puglia, peachily ripe and
piqued by citrus edging; 12.5% alcohol.

9 **Specially Selected**
Castellore Soave Classico 2020 £5.49
Smart-looking bottle for this proper crowd-pleaser from
the famed if arguably now-unfashionable Veronese DOC.
Attractive green-hinting pale-gold colour, blossomy-citrus
nose and perky crisp white fruits edged with grapefruit
tang, lively and fresh; very easy to like; 12.5% alcohol.
The price looks ridiculously low but this is definitely the
real thing.

8 **Castellore Pecorino 2020** £5.49
From the Terre di Chieti IGT in the Abruzzo, a dry but
lush and grassy aperitif wine of wholesome freshness;
12.5% alcohol.

WHITE WINES

NEW ZEALAND

🍷 **9** **Freeman's Bay Pinot Gris 2020** £6.49

Don't expect a Kiwi version of Italy's Pinot Grigio – this is a serious wine, pleasingly pungent with smoky-spicy notes to the bright orchard fruit and a thought-provoking fullness of flavour, quite dry but with honey allusions; 13% alcohol. Nice partner for tricky menus including salads, Asian dishes and assertive seafood.

PORTUGAL

🍷 **8** **Mimo Moutinho Portuguese Loureiro 2020** £6.49

'A flagship grape turned into the branco of Portugal' proclaims the graffiti-like bold text on the front label of this likeable new wine (well, new to me). The grape in question is Loureiro, which I'm prepared to bet is unknown to all but the most avid oenophiles but is a key variety in the dry white wine of the Minho Valley, vinho verde. And that's what this is: zingy-fresh with a trace of condition or 'petillance', floral and citrus-tangy with delicate ripe white fruit and naturally dry; 11.5% alcohol.

ROMANIA

🍷 **8** **Dealuri Feteasca Regala 2020** £4.99

New (to me anyway) venture into Romanian wine for Aldi. A soft but fresh party wine from indigenous Feteasca grape showing discreetly floral apple-pear fruit with a well-judged lift of acidity; 11.5% alcohol. Nice package.

SPARKLING WINES

FRANCE

🍷 **10** **Crémant de Jura 2018** £8.49

From sublime hill country east of Burgundy, this long-term Aldi favourite fizz constantly morphs its bottle shape and labelling but remains a consistent treat and bargain. Pure ripe sweet-apple Chardonnay in a rush of persistent bubbles, quite delightful and fresh; 11.5% alcohol.

SPARKLING WINES

**8 Veuve Monsigny
No. 111 Champagne Brut**   **£12.99**
It's decent stuff, artfully ripe in its apple-pie savour,
lemony fresh but not green; 12% alcohol. The price is
keen but you'd do better with the serious-quality house
champagnes of Sainsbury or Tesco on promo at only a
pound or two more.

**9 Veuve Monsigny Champagne Rosé
No. 111 Brut**   **£16.99**
Pink champagne is invariably costlier than its white
counterparts but this one merits the lift by being
exceptionally good (and good value) in its own right.
Fine copper-bright colour, big sweet strawberry with
lemon zest nose, generous small-bubble rush and gleeful
summer-soft-berry juiciness to the racy flavour; 12.5%
alcohol.

8 Costellore Prosecco Rosé Extra Dry   **£6.49**
Tasted live on Channel 4's *Sunday Brunch*, this was a
hit. We all agreed that its perky colour, strawberry scent
and fresh lift made it a step up from bog-standard white
prosecco, and that the price makes it a bargain; 11%
alcohol.

8 Organic Prosecco   **£7.99**
The label description Extra Dry is untypically accurate
on this decent, lively apple-and-pear-juicy, elderflower-
scented confection; 11.5% alcohol.

FRANCE

ITALY

Asda

Well, they've done it now. Walmart sold most of its shares in Asda to the Issa brothers, tycoons of the petrol-forecourt business, for £6,800,000,000 in 2021. Major changes have taken place in Asda management and to in-store arrangements, and the future for the chain is about as certain as it is for the petrol-forecourt business, given that within less than a decade, sales of new cars using petrol or diesel will be outlawed in Britain.

No doubt Mohsin and Zuber Issa have a plan. Whether it includes wine sales is an open question. They are reported to be devout Muslims and have so far sold no alcohol in any of their petrol-station shops. I have enjoyed the rumours about the possible contracting-out of Asda's beer, wine and spirits, but can only imagine how the whole thing will turn out in the long run.

For the moment, I have to say, Asda looks unbeatable on price for wines. My first foray to buy new-season wines in 2021 took me to a biggish branch where there's usually a pretty decent selection. I wasn't disappointed and, as it happens, there was a 25%-off deal if you bought six or more bottles, any mix. I bought 16 bottles and paid about £80. Yup, that's a fiver a piece. And these were proper wines. Quite a few were on 'Rollback', Asda's curious name for individual promos. So a wine usually £7.50 and down to £6.00 could be had for £4.50. Now that's a deal.

And some of the wines were pretty good. On this first outing and a couple of follow-ups, I found that the range has continued the process of narrowing begun a few years ago, but that there are still interesting own-label wines under the 'Extra Special' heading and a few quality brands, some of them new to me. I have given maximum scores to recently listed Dr L Riesling from Germany and to a French Midi red (new to me) at just £6.

Yes, price is a major draw. Large numbers of the wines appear to be on individual discount at any one time, and Asda seems now to have adopted the 25%-off-any-six offers that have been such a key feature at Sainsbury's and Tesco for as long as I can remember.

RED WINES

ARGENTINA

 7 Extra Special San Juan Malbec 2020 £7.00
Decent if one-dimensional brambly number – not a patch on the memorable 2019 vintage despite a price drop from last year; 13.5% alcohol.

CHILE

**0 Extra Special Valle de
Colchagua Carmenère 2019** £6.50
Absolute stinker. Dull and dead. Perhaps a bad bottle? The 2018 was delicious. What a difference a vintage can make.

FRANCE

**10 Grignan-les-Adhémar
Cuvée Traditionelle 2019** £6.00
Astoundingly good not-quite-Côtes-du-Rhône AC formerly known as Coteaux du Tricastin; delightfully weighted, juicy with red fruits, gently spicy and altogether wholesome and satisfying (14% alcohol), easily comparable to good-quality CdR. The AC of Grignan-les-Aldhémar, to quote the back label, 'produces some of the most undervalued wines in the entire region'. This one totally makes the case. One reservation: horrible plastic cork; maybe it saves a centime or two.

ITALY

**8 Extra Special Montepulciano
d'Abruzzo 2019** £5.50
Easy-weighted juicy-bouncy raspberry-brambly bright young thing of vigorous charm with a good dry edge to the purple fruit and a nice cut for sticky pasta dishes; good everyday example of the distinctive Abruzzo Monty style and jolly cheap; 13% alcohol.

RED WINES

ITALY

🍷 **8** **Extra Special Primitivo 2019** £6.50
Strong, vigorous, intense raspberry-blackcurrant spicy
rustic Puglian food red at a keen price that hangs together
well for drinking with highly flavoured dishes from chilli
to cheesy bakes; good acidity, brisk finish; 13.5% alcohol.

🍷 **7** **Burdizzo Chianti Riserva 2016** £7.00
Very bad cork that was almost impenetrably compacted
and broke halfway out – note to producer. But the wine
was unaffected apart from the cork motes floating in the
first pour. This aside, it's a decent bottle of Chianti with
recognisable cherry-raspberry juiciness and brisk grip but
lighter, leaner, than last year's very enjoyable 2015 in
spite of two years in oak as a *riserva* wine; 12.5% alcohol.

🍷 **9** **Villa Vincini Gran Rosso 2020** £8.00
Ooh, what a comfort this cushiony curiosity is. A mere
IGT (regional generic) Veneto from an unlikely mix of
Merlot with Corvina, the grape of Valpolicella and
its ripasso variations, it combines sweet black cherry
ripeness with a suggestion of mocha with trim Italian grip
to make a throughly versatile food match; 14% alcohol.
A very likeable contrivance in a fun-looking package (like
the reassuring red seal) that performs equally well on
reopening the day after.

RED WINES

ITALY

🍷 9 Orbitali Amarone Della Valpolicella 2016   £16.00

Coffee, bitter chocolate and, I swear, prunes, are all to be detected among the stygian savours of this friendly monster, contrived from cherry-sweet, sun-baked blackberry-pie Valpolicella boosted with concentrated must and deliciously balanced between plushness and abrasion. It goes with any kind of sticky, saucy Italian food and adds heady delight to special occasions; 14.5% alcohol. Love the overwrought label and the price is fair – I paid not much over a tenner on promo.

PORTUGAL

🍷 8 Bodacious Vinho 2019   £6.50

Light in colour and heft but not without intensity, this is very Portuguese: cinnamon and clove in the brambly blackcurrant sweet-but-neat fruit it has good cut to partner oily fish, sticky pasta or exotic rice dishes; 13.5% alcohol. I think the presentation is awful and the contrived tale of Bodacious – 'the greatest bull ever to buck' – very silly. And the anthropomorphic assertion that this wine is 'fierce, ferocious and untameable' is, well, a load of old bull. Like the wine right enough, though.

🍷 9 Extra Special Dão 2019   £6.50

Nice bottling of this once-better-known regional red which has earthy appeal, good colour intensity, middling in weight, healthy in black fruit with elderberry and raspberry to the fore, easy plumpness and neat finish; tastes of itself; 13% alcohol. Needs food: rice dishes, sardines, you name it.

RED WINES

Asda

PORTUGAL

🍷 8 **Extra Special Douro 2019** £6.50
Clear bright label and immediately likeable weight and
savour in this recognisable table wine from port grapes;
13.5% alcohol. Surprising that it comes in a screwcap
bottle (albeit one emblazoned with Asda's Extra Special
marque) as Portugal is the chief wine-cork-producing
nation of the world.

ROMANIA

🍷 8 **Wine Atlas Feteasca Neagra 2020** £5.25
From Romania's leading winery Cramele Recas, founded
in 1447, collectivised under communist hegemony from
1948 to 1990 but now back in capitalist clutches, this
attractively packaged indigenous party red is a sprightly-
brambly middleweight of real charm; its sweet summer
red fruit is balanced by easy citrus acidity to make a
distinctive style you could enjoy fridge cool on outdoor
days; 12% alcohol.

SPAIN

🍷 8 **Extra Special Old Vine Garnacha 2019** £6.00
Dependable annual bargain from Cariñena region of
Aragon is roundly ripe and pepper-spiced with a minty
perkiness and easy tannin; 14.5% alcohol.

PINK WINES

FRANCE

9 Le Cellier de Saint Louis Coteaux Varois
Provence Rosé 2019   £6.99

It might be the 2020 by now, but the 2019 was even better than the 2018 (spotted here last year) and usefully down in price from £8.50. Grenache-based pale copper pink with floral-citrus pong, crisp redcurrant-raspberry savour, very fresh and very dry; 13% alcohol. It says Provence on the label, which usually hikes the price, even though Provence has more real prestige as a holiday destination than as a wine region, but this wine is from the neighbouring, less chi-chi Var, where the wines can really shine. So there.

WHITE WINES

AUSTRALIA

7 Extra Special Barossa Valley
Chardonnay 2020   £7.50

Hmm. It's not that special – rather sweet either from the partial barrique fermentation mentioned in the blurb or retained sugar, a pineappley note in the fruit and 13.5% alcohol. I realise Australia has a lot of wine to offload, but for this money we should expect better.

FRANCE

9 Picpoul de Pinet 2020   £7.00

Nice brisk sea-air-fresh spin on this plausibly popular Mediterranean formula. There's a sherbetty zing to the long green-apple fruit and lifting limey acidity; really well contrived at a sensible price; 13% alcohol. I read somewhere that picpoul wines used to be diverted into the manufacture of local vermouth, before finding its current vogue. Just like all those chi-chi dry white Sicilians, once drowned in the murky midden of Marsala.

WHITE WINES

🍷 **10** **Dr L Riesling 2019** £7.00

Very relieved to find this superb moselle still at Asda, who took it over from Sainsbury's last year in the midst of the failed merger talks. It's as zesty, minerally and green-apple crisp as ever with a twist of sherbet ripeness amid the racy Riesling rush; 8.5% alcohol. Top value.

🍷 **8** **Diverso Falanghina 2018** £7.50

From Beneventano in the Campania region of southwest Italy, a zingy aperitif dry wine with notes of greengage and grapefruit in the aroma and the addition of pear and even pineapple in the flavour; fresh, fanciful stuff and fun; 12.5% alcohol

🍷 **8** **Tukituki Marlborough**
Sauvignon Blanc 2020 £7.00

I like the name (it means 'smash' in Maori) and equally like the wine: big bloom of Granny Smith, peapod, seagrass and lime followed up by generous fruit along the same lines; 12.5% alcohol. It's characterful and well priced.

🍷 **9** **Wine Atlas Feteasca Regala 2020** £5.25

Artful aromatic off-dry white from Romania's own 'Royal Maiden' grape variety – genuinely distinctive, balancing peachy plumpness with redcurrant and crisp-apple savours; 11.5% alcohol. It's good to see the attractively labelled Wine Atlas series still, just, on track at Asda, delivering real vinous variety at economy-class prices.

WHITE WINES

SOUTH AFRICA

8 Extra Special Chardonnay 2020 £5.50
Friendly scents of peach and pineapple from this softly
obliging Atlantic-facing Western Cape wine, making
the most of its natural-tasting sweet-apple Chardonnay
ripeness (13.5% alcohol). Very safe bet at this price.

SPAIN

**8 Extra Special Palacio de
Vivero Rueda 2020** £5.00
Brightly tangy and crisp dry white from excellent Rueda
DO of Castille from Verdejo grapes delivering hallmark
apple-crisp, lemony freshness and lingering savours; 13%
alcohol.

9 Extra Special Albariño Rias Baixas 2020 £9.00
Phew. You get a proper blast of sea air and briny tang
from the nose of this big yellow wine from Spain's
salty Atlantic coast. It's terrific stuff, needs mussels or
smoked fish, and sets a good standard for this rightly
admired style; 13% alcohol. Not cheap at shelf price
but I got mine on promo for a lot less.

SPARKLING WINES

ENGLAND

9 Extra Special English Sparkling Brut £21.00
Clearly modelled on the champagne formula – same grape
varieties and production method – this Home Counties
pretender is entirely convincing with its alluring colour,
bakery whiffs and ripe but crisp orchard fruits conveyed
on a deluxe stream of tiny bubbles; I think it's the same
bottling I tasted last year, from the 2015 harvest, and it's
mellowing very nicely indeed; 12% alcohol.

SPARKLING WINES

FRANCE

🍷 9 **Extra Special Crémant de Loire Brut** £9.00
Glad to see Asda persisting with this seductively sparkling
(*crémant* translates as 'creaming') fizz from Chenin Blanc
grapes delivering a distinctive balance of ripe sweet apple
with citrus zing; 12% alcohol.

The Co-operative

 It has 6,000 or so outlets throughout the country and all of them, as far as I know, sell wine. My local market town branch, however, sells fewer than half of the wines recommended here. I had to travel to far-distant destinations to buy most of this year's selections.

But I don't begrudge it. The Co-op's wine range is simply extraordinary. Larger branches sell as enterprising a collection of sensibly priced bottles as any other supermarket barring only Waitrose. Consider the choice from France. As well as good-value middle-ranking clarets (eg Château Beaumont), there are brilliantly chosen reds from Pécharmant, Pic St Loup, Saint-Chinian and Saumur, all appellations otherwise thinly represented in the supermarket sector.

Italy scores equally well for red wines, and whites, too. And New World wines are looking stronger year by year. Besides the Fairtrade wines from South America and South Africa with which the Co-op has long led the way in UK retailing, this year I've been pleased to find really good-value bargain Australian wines and, under the Co-op's still-limited 'Irresistible' own-label brand, a memorable Pinot Noir from Chile. They are all here in the modest selection that follows. And I should reiterate the advice that should your local branch not have what you're looking for, you can resort to the computer. Not to order wines for home delivery as the Co-op doesn't do that sort of thing (amazingly in these times) but to locate the nearest outlet stocking your choice.

Go to the Co-operative home page online, click on Co-op Food and then on Wines. There's a Find a Wine search box. Type in the name, go to the 'find this product' box, put your postcode in and you'll get a list of the nearest branches stocking it.

I promise you'll find it worth the trouble.

RED WINES

AUSTRALIA

8 Andrew Peace Shiraz 2020 £5.50

It says 'ripe black fruit and delicate cherry flavours' on the utilitarian front label of this wholesome Victoria State varietal by Andrew Peace, a dependable and long-term supplier to the Co-op. It's as cheap as proper Aussie wine gets, and tastes just as described; 13.5% alcohol.

CHILE

9 Co-op Irresistible 30° Pinot Noir 2019 £8.00

Exemplary Casablanca Pinot: elegant but muscular (14% alcohol) with slinky pull to its earthy raspberry juiciness. It's a proper indicator of Chile's distinctive spin on the great grape of Burgundy, a lush match for game and poultry, and a gift at this price. Maker Viña Indomita is based amid spectacular Andean valleys at 30 degrees south of the Equator, in case you were wondering about the name.

FRANCE

8 Beaujolais AOP £5.50

This very simply labelled non-vintage screwcap everyday wine at a sensible price is properly juicy and bouncy: square-deal Beaujolais to enjoy any time, including gently chilled on warmer days; 12.5% alcohol.

9 Les Hauts de Saint Martin Saint-Chinian 2019 £7.75

From the redoubtable Cave de Roquebrun co-operative, producer of numerous delicious wines made under the St Chinian AC, this is a typically warm, garrigue-spicy Syrah-based food red (cassoulet, sausages etc) full of signature fruits-of-the-forest savours, hearty (13.5% alcohol) and trim with easy tannin. 'This wine will age beautifully for up to 3 years' boasts the back label, and I can well believe it.

RED WINES

FRANCE

🍷 **10** **Domaine des Ormes Saumur 2018** £8.00

It's a great comfort that the Co-op persists with this lovely Loire wine. Made by two brothers with the reassuringly Gallic names Pascal and François Champion it's textbook Saumur red, delicate in purply hue, distinctively scented with sun-baked blueberry tangy ripeness and jangling with bright, juicy red fruits made delightfully abrasive by a lush leafiness; 12.5% alcohol. Light but not unsubstantial in heft, it responds very well to moderate chilling. Paradoxically perhaps, it mellows beautifully with age. The 2016 was at perfect pitch in 2021 (and I did find some in a Co-op as late as May). The price is nugatory – invest for now and later.

🍷 **9** **Clos Montalbanie Pécharmant 2018** £8.00

Pécharmant is a pocket AC of good repute amid the wider and generally ordinary appellation of Bergerac, neighbouring Bordeaux and cultivating the same grape varieties. This one is terrific, intensely maroon coloured, generous with bramble-elderberry-leafy aromas and vigorously emphatic in its black-fruit flavours; it's wholesome and I guess unoaked but smooth and long, well-developed already and 14.5% alcohol. It's like classy claret, but somehow more bucolic. Smart package, keen price.

🍷 **9** **Domaine Les Grandes Costes Pic St Loup 2017** £15.25

I thought the Co-op had dropped this magnificent Languedoc special-occasion red, but it's back on shelf, from what is clearly a jolly good 2017 vintage. Impressive opaque colour, terrific bloom of spicy Syrah aroma, opulent silky dark fruits with roasty mulberry savours; 14.5% alcohol. It's worth decanting a wine as big as this, and it will no doubt develop for years if 'cellared'.

RED WINES

FRANCE

8 Château Beaumont 2017 £16.00
Beaumont is a noble estate of Bordeaux's Haut-Médoc, classified *cru bourgeois* but making wines that rival far more elevated growths fetching prices several times higher. Good cassis fruit and cedar savour are here in this still-developing wine from the troubled 2017 vintage. It's a good effort but needs time; 14% alcohol.

ITALY

10 Palladino Biferno Rosso Riserva 2017 £7.00
Phew. I'm relieved to report yet another very likeable vintage for this curiosity from Molise, just south of the Abruzzi in Italy's east midlands. There's the right juicy perfume of Montepulciano grapes with a good measure of sweet even chocolatey baked darker fruit from Aglianico grapes, the other half of this unusual blend. Plumped with oak contact and benefitting from time in bottle, it's seductively ripe (13% alcohol) with proper friendly tannin at the finish. Great pasta match and down in price from last year's £8.

7 Villa Garducci Merlot 2020 £7.00
Who drinks Italian Merlot? This Veneto IGT (generic) is made by Fratelli Martini, so I took a chance. It's light in colour and weight, cherry sweet on nose and palate with a little lick of caramel but reasonable balance. Italian Merlot all the way you might say but easy and inoffensive; 12% alcohol.

RED WINES

ITALY

🍷 **10** **Vanita Puglia Negroamaro 2019** £7.30

How could any wine live up to the magnificence of a label such as this? Well, this one does. The ornamentation of the baroque heraldic entablature is easily matched by the nuances of the chocolate-prune-blackberry fruit, sublime spicy ripeness and long, tannin-defined balanced savours. Its ideal acidity cuts like a blade through the stickiest and starchiest of Italian dishes; 14% alcohol.

🍷 **8** **Irresistible Barbera**
d'Asti Superiore 2018 £7.50

Near-black in colour, juicy but edgy and darkly savoury typically bouncy blueberry-bramble-cherry bright Piedmontese wine with woof (14.5% alcohol) and grip comes in a smart screwtop package, with the useful label advice to try it with barbecues.

PINK WINES

SPAIN

🍷 **8** **Cune Rioja Rosado 2020** £8.50

By Spanish pink-wine standards, this is discreetly coloured, a restrained pale salmon, but you get plenty of strawberry perfume and red-fruit savours in the run-up to the brisk, dry edge, very fresh and lively (12.5% alcohol).

WHITE WINES

AUSTRALIA

🍷 **9** **Andrew Peace Chardonnay 2020** £5.50

Far more fruit and interest packed into this Victoria State wine than I'd expected at the price: good gold colour, pleasing brassica vigour beside the sweet-apple near-unctuous plump style lifted with mixed citrus end flavours, perfectly dry but not without a suggestion of richness; an artful contrivance; 13% alcohol.

WHITE WINES

FRANCE

8 Picpoul de Pinet Paul Mas 2020 £7.50
Crisp new vintage – a very successful harvest, I hear –
for this popular Mediterranean aperitif/fish partner from
Languedoc titan Jean Claude Mas. It's very fresh indeed
but with much interest from nectarine and sweetly ripe
orchard fruits twanged with friendly grapefruit acidity;
12.5% alcohol.

ITALY

10 Vanita Grillo 2020 £7.00
The sensational heraldic labelling by no means oversells
this magnificent Sicilian dry wine. It has a gorgeous lemon-
gold, sea-green-tinged colour, enigmatic brassica-citrus
nose and nectarine-grapefruit zing overlying tropical fruit
lushness – a clue to the nature of the Grillo grape, once
employed only in the elaboration of sticky marsala, now
riding high among Sicily's new wave of dry white wines;
13% alcohol. I'm prepared to forgive the cheesy slogan
printed on the side of the cork: 'Made with love'.

NEW ZEALAND

**8 Irresistible Marlborough
Pinot Grigio 2020** £7.50
Modelled more on the Pinot Gris of Alsace than the PG
of Italy, this has friendly spice and smokiness alongside
the apple-pear freshness and citrus lift; 13% alcohol.
Hardy perennial that scores for interest (not always a PG
feature) and makes a versatile food match – exotic menus
included.

WHITE WINES

New Zealand

🍷 **9** **The Ned Sauvignon Blanc 2020** £9.50
Tasted in distinguished company on Channel 4's *Sunday
Brunch*, this perennial favourite was universally admired.
I'd planned to claim its name had some connection to
yours truly, but sensibly chickened out. Just as well, as
the programme's producer turned out to be a dedicated
fan, and everyone else seemed familar with it. That'll
teach me: I thought it was my little secret discovery,
but it's on sale in most of the big supermarkets, it turns
out. And yet it's a truly individual wine full of zest and
glittering Sauvignon character; 13% alcohol. Frequently
discounted at the Co-op and the several other chains that
stock it.

South Africa

🍷 **8** **Co-op Irresistible Fairtrade
Sauvignon Blanc 2020** £6.00
Full of familiar gooseberry-grassy flavours but gentle on
the acidity, an agreeable Cape wine to please conservative
tastes; 12% alcohol. Good value at £6 and I've seen it
reduced to £5. I hope the discount is not deducted from
the Fairtrade scheme's share of the ante.

🍷 **8** **Fruit Orchestra Chenin
Blanc Viogner 2020** £8.00
The staves featuring in this wine are not for once the
components of the oak barrel, but the decorative theme of
the label design. And all very lyrical it looks. Doesn't taste
bad either, even though the duet of the constituent grape
varieties, both known for their soft if not sweet styles
might seem counterintuitive rather than contrapuntal.
Ho ho ho hmm. The success here is in the balance. You
get the expected lush white fruit suggesting apricot, sweet
melon and white peach and it's all brightly lifted by citrus
even grapefruit acidity into, yes, a harmonious outcome.
I liked it, especially at £6 paid on promo; 13% alcohol.

WHITE WINES

SOUTH AFRICA

🍷 **9** **Vergelegen Sauvignon Blanc 2020** £10.00

Just how does the Co-op do it? Vergelegen (it means 'far away place' in Afrikaans), one of the Cape's oldest (1790) and grandest wine estates, is in partnership with the Co-op to make this exciting Fairtrade wine, lush with minerally gooseberry-grassy fruit, sunnily ripe and full of character; 13.5% alcohol.

FORTIFIED WINES

PORTUGAL

🍷 **8** **Sandeman Fine White Port** £10.00

Good to see the Co-op persisting with this oddity in its wasp-yellow presentation box. White port (well, amber really) is an everyday aperitif at home in Portugal, served ice cold, often on the rocks, and even mixed with tonic. This, from the excellent Sandeman of 'grocer's port' infamy, is a fine example: sweet in the port manner but rich with preserved-fruit flavours and brisk at the finish; 19.5% alcohol.

SPARKLING WINES

ENGLAND

🍷 **10** **Balfour 1503 Foxwood Cuvee** £17.00

Asked by Channel 4's *Sunday Brunch* programme to pick my favourite English sparkling wine I was happy to be able to recommend this one. It's from Kentish vineyards planted 20 years ago with Chardonnay and Pinot Noir, the grapes that go into champagne, and it's made by the same complicated method. It's well-coloured, banging with tiny bubbles and joyously alive with yeasty aromas and long ripe white-fruit flavours, very dry and very fresh with 11.5% alcohol. It's exclusive (I'm told) to the Co-op and fairly priced. I've tried English sparklers costing twice as much that are less enjoyable.

SPARKLING WINES

🍷 **9** **Les Pionniers Champagne Brut** £19.00

It's a poorly kept secret, according to the Co-op, that its house champagne Les Pionniers (French for The Pioneers who started the Co-op in 1844) is made by Piper Heidsieck. I am more of a fan of the Co-op's version than of the Piper rendering, especially in light of the price difference, and commend this distinctive lemon-meringue-pie scented champagne for its balance between ripe sweet-apple fruit and tangy citrus lift, all carried along on a creamily persisting mousse; 12% alcohol.

FRANCE

The Co-operative

Lidl

 Good old Lidl. It's an endearing name for what can seem a quaint organisation. The stores I have visited all appear to operate on a common principle of barely controlled chaos. Carefully considered shopping lists are redundant. If I can find half of what I've hoped for on the basis of previous visits, that counts as a success. And then there's the matter of getting into the right checkout queue. The wrong move can portend a numbing stasis.

This is, of course, an observation based entirely on personal experience. I'm not much of a shopper at the best times and am as capable as anyone else of leaving the list behind on the kitchen table anyway.

Which brings me to the wines. The core range at Lidl is by far the shortest permanent-stock list of the ten retailers featured in this book. Years ago, when I regularly attended Lidl's jolly wine tastings for the press, I was perpetually assured by the buyers that the core list was on the point of being radically expanded. But it hasn't happened.

Instead, the main thrust of the Lidl offering is the Wine Tour. Six times a year, new selections of up to 30 wines are distributed across the stores, remaining on sale as long as stocks last. Which might not be very long. There are often interesting and good-value wines, all tasted and rated by Master of Wine and all-round good egg Richard Bampfield, whose 'Bampfield points' out of 100 are clearly displayed on the shelves.

Trouble is, in the antediluvian context of *The Best Wines in the Supermarkets*, any remarks I have might have to make about these Wine Tour ephemera will be of no purpose. By the time you're plunging into these pages, the tour has moved on.

And so to this year's little selection, about a dozen from the current vintages of established regulars. Decent wines, every one, as much for their quality and interest as for their price. Curiously, while I am well aware Lidl undercuts the competition with its prices for most merchandise, I have never observed that this applies to the wine range.

RED WINES

CHILE

🍷 8 **Malbec Reserva Privada 2019**   £5.99
For the money, a nice buy from Chile's prodigious Central Valley, darkly savoury with detectable Malbec grip and spice; 13.5% alcohol. A rare highlight of the never-expanding Lidl core range.

SPAIN

🍷 9 **Baturrica Tarragona Gran Reserva 2014**   £5.49
Another triumphant vintage for this formidable perennial succeeding last year's rather tough 2012 with an arguably more rounded, black-fruited, vanilla-hinting, pungent and peppery Catalan pensioner. It's 12% alcohol compared to 2012's 13% and I sense a less overheated nature to the fruit. Really not bad at all and very cheap for what it is in all its gaudy attire of wire cage and avant-garde decoration. Lidl says it goes well with cottage pie. Chilli, I'd venture.

🍷 8 **Cepa Lebrel Rioja Reserva 2015**   £5.49
Authentic reserva with an improved new-look label design at no loss to its consistent value. Lively black fruit ripeness and a vanilla lick from barrel-age, at a low price for the rightly rated Rioja region, which had a particularly good vintage in 2015; 13.5% alcohol.

WHITE WINES

CHILE

🍷 8 **Cimarosa Pedro Jimenez 2019**   £4.29
The Pedro Ximenes (PX) grape of Spain is mainly recognised as a sweetening agent in dark sherry. Here, from the Andean foothills of Chile it makes a dry, spicy and really quite refreshing pale white wine of some character; 12% alcohol. A dependable Lidl perennial cheapie.

WHITE WINES

FRANCE

🍷 8 **Chablis 2019** £9.99

In newspaper advertisements, Lidl describes this wine as 'French Chablis'. It's a nostalgic reminder of the days when the great wine names of France were regularly hijacked by upstarts from Australia, the USA and pre-EU Spain, cheerfully passing off their generic wines as bargain versions of the classics. Lidl is doing its bit to recall the good old buccaneering days. Lidl French Chablis has featured in these pages since its 2012 vintage and I'm happy to report that the 2019 is up to snuff: attractive colour in which you can at least imagine the Chablis 'gold shot with green' hue, flinty aroma and crisp, limey mineral Chardonnay fruit; 12.5% alcohol.

NEW ZEALAND

🍷 9 **Cimarosa Marlborough Sauvignon Blanc 2020** £5.79

They've changed the name from Cimarosa New Zealand SB and reduced the price fractionally from £5.99 but I swear it's the same tangy gooseberry wine as before and dependably one of the best bargains on the Lidl core list; 12.5% alcohol.

SOUTH AFRICA

🍷 8 **Fairtrade Sauvignon Blanc 2020** £5.49

Good cause and good value from the Western Cape's troubled 2020 vintage (the main problem being the South African government's arguably capricious banning of alcohol sales in response to the Covid crisis) in this brisk and grassy-zingy goosegog refresher at a keen price; 13% alcohol. I believe it's a core line. Hope so.

WHITE WINES

SOUTH AFRICA

🍷 8 **Fairtrade Chenin Blanc 2020**   £5.99
I reckon this is a core list item and it deserves to be.
Daisy-fresh with an eager floral pong and likeable Cape
Chenin combo of tang and tropical fruit flavour; 12.5%
alcohol.

SPAIN

🍷 8 **Cepa Lebrel Rioja Blanco 2018**   £4.49
Possibly a recent addition to the core list, the bottle I
bought in summer 2021 was the 2018 vintage, which
should have been superseded by the time you're reading
this. The point is that even at three years old it was
pleasingly fresh as well as ripely white-Rioja-like; 12.5%
alcohol.

🍷 8 **CEO Godello Monterrei 2019**   £8.49
In last year's edition I speculated that this keen dry wine
from Galicia might be a candidate for continuity – and it
was duly included in a Lidl's 'wine tour' display in 2021,
in the same 2019 vintage but up in price from £7.99 to
£8.49. It's still worth it: fresh and lush with a seaside tang
and lashings of ripe orchard fruit; 12.5% alcohol. If a
2020 follows, take the plunge.

SPARKLING WINES

FRANCE

🍷 9 **Crémant de Loire Brut**   £8.49
The smart new livery for this dependable perennial is nicely
done, and the wine is as good as ever: creamily foaming,
brisk lemon-meringue aromas and fruit, certainly dry
but with a sneaky lush honeyed note from Chenin Blanc
grapes. Not cheap, just downright delicious; 12% alcohol.

Majestic

I am really quite excited about Majestic. For years, the 200-outlet 'warehouse' chain has seemed buffeted by corporate contortions amid a series of weird takeovers, name changes and even rumours of extinction. But now, in spite of these terrible times of pandemic, the nation's last-surviving high-street merchant looks entirely back in business.

In the absence of any chance to taste the range at an organised event, I sallied forth in summer 2021 to my nearest Majestic store in Yeovil, Somerset. I had with me a carefully thought-out shopping list worked up after much consideration of the website, which amply describes the many hundreds of wines on offer. You can order online for home delivery, but I wanted to see inside a branch.

It was smart and orderly, much more so than in the days of the messy, piled-high warehouse emporia of old. There was an attentive and clearly knowledgeable young chap at the desk, and there were still supermarket trolleys – the original pretext I used for including Majestic in this guide.

You need to take your time. I had numerous wines to pick out and needed help to find some of them (grateful thanks to my daughter Lydia). But I felt at home because there were a good few old favourites still available, such as Santa Rita from Chile, for which

Majestic was a pioneer stockist, plus good Beaujolais (always a feature here) and my favourite Verona ripasso La Casetta.

Majestic has long done a range of own-label wines under the brand 'Definition' but I skipped most of those (except the fab half of Sauternes) in quest of new discoveries. I did like the own-label The Guv'nor red from Spain – top marks for that – and found an astoundingly good old Mosel auslese at a sensible price, prompting memories of the time when Majestic's founding wine buyer Tony Mason, who sadly died in 2021, used to ferret out parcels of these wonders from the estates of his contacts in Germany.

I mentioned sensible prices. They're not all sensible at Majestic. Each wine has two: list price and mix-six price. If you buy any six wines at once, you pay the latter, qualifying for discounts somewhere between ten and 25 per cent. The prices I quote are all mix-six. Buying wine from Majestic in smaller quantities, either online or in person, surely cannot make sense.

RED WINES

⟨8⟩ Santa Rita Reserva Especial
120 Merlot 2020 £7.49

CHILE

A journey down memory lane: I visited the Santa Rita estate in 1984, admired the wines and was impressed when Majestic (then, like Chile, a new player in the trade) took them on. This current Merlot is a testament to Santa Rita's consistency: ripe black-cherry aromas and fruits, artful vanilla, piquant berry juiciness, gentle grip, natural and poised; 13% alcohol. Chile, and Majestic, have both come a long way.

⟨9⟩ Auberge Petite Pierre Corbières 2018 £6.99
Convincingly inky-spicy Mediterranean garrigue red with the warm muscular tension associated with the appellation; it's rather deluxe, presumably some oak contact, and very tidy at the finish; 13.5% alcohol. Class act for a wine at this price from Majestic – redemptive, I call it.

⟨8⟩ Alain Grignon Carignan Sélection
Vieilles Vignes 2020 £6.99

FRANCE

Perky brambly new-vintage Pays d'Hérault; youthful maroon in colour but balanced between focused ripeness and grip in a thoroughly grown-up style; immediately likeable adaptable food red – fish as well as meat – from vines reputedly 50 years old; 12.5% alcohol.

⟨10⟩ Loron Beaujolais 2020 £7.99
The Loron family have been making wine in Beaujolais since 1711 but I can't hold that against them: this is everything you could hope for – lovely, purple-juicy, bouncing, eager but intensely ripe and long fruit bomb in the best tradition; 13% alcohol. Even the price is right.

RED WINES

FRANCE

9 Paul Jaboulet Aîné Parallèle 45 Côtes du Rhône 2019 £10.99

Absolutely dependable classic on great form in yet another fabled vintage for the Rhône. Brimming with ripe and savoury spicily dark fruits all in seemingly effortless balance; 14% alcohol. A new feature (to me) this year is the bee-symbol signalling of the organic status of Jaboulet wine. Jolly good.

8 Domaine Pardon Juliénas Les Mouilles 2020 £10.99

New wine from a picturesque *cru*, already lusciously good notwithstanding the back-label advice that you could hold on to it for four or five years more; just seems like a really joyful Beaujolais to me; 13.5% alcohol.

ITALY

8 Primo Rosso Appassimento 2018 £7.99

Same vintage as last year's and the mix-six price is down from £8.99 to £7.99. It's a bit of a brute: deep maroon colour, blast of baked black-fruit ripeness on the nose and a lot of spicy matching flavour with 14.5% alcohol. Proper deep south (Puglia) winter red for highly-flavoured meaty dishes.

7 Domodo Negroamaro 2019 £7.99

This light but flavoursome Puglian generic wine from fast-emerging local Negroamaro grape has hallmark brambly juiciness and a friendly rasp at the edge to balance the sweetness; 12% alcohol. Reportedly a top-seller at Majestic, but at £8.99 list, not exactly a snip.

RED WINES

🍷 **8** **Lifili Salice Salentino 2017** £8.99

Nicely presented, mild-mannered, sweetly savoury, cherry-violet toffee-tinted maturing smoothie from Puglia's Salento region's best-known DOP; 13.5% alcohol. It improved noticeably after being reopened next day, so do decant. I liked the back label encomium about wine 'born in old family vineyards managed with female passion' but was less convinced by the parsimonious £1 mix-six off the £9.99 list price.

🍷 **8** **Corte Ferro Nerello Frappato 2019** £9.99

Sicilian spaghetti red by lyrical-sounding producer Caruso & Minini has a sort of deep-magenta colour, cheerful black-cherry hoot and bouncy vigorous hedgerow fruit as you might expect from the grape combo – easy and stimulating in style, wholesomely crisp and bright but not without heft at 13.5% alcohol. Plenty of pizzazz here, and not just in the label design.

🍷 **0** **Dolcetto D'Alba de Forville 2019** £9.99

The horrible polymer cork was the first sign of trouble. This was a shockingly bad wine, dilute, oxidised, lifeless – but presumably not 'corked'. Disgracefully bad, and at a list price of £11.99, beyond a joke.

🍷 **9** **Nero Oro Riserva 2017** £11.99

Cool designery-looking package for this serious Sicilian reveals old-fashioned virtues of assured blackcurrant and plum intensity enrobed (forgive me) in a chocolate and vanilla richness imparted by oak contact; it's a thoroughly Sicilian wine, spicy and gripping, from star local grape variety Nero d'Avola, redolent of the plush leather upholstery of the *capo di capi's* shiny new roadster; 14% alcohol.

RED WINES

ITALY

🍷 **9** **Domini Veneti Valpolicella Ripasso**
Classico Superiore La Casetta 2017   **£14.99**
Very pleased to find this lovely vintage still on offer. It's silkily succulent and minty with that peculiarly seductive intensity of ripasso (see A Wine Vocabulary pg 149) with the unusual inclusion of *recioto* grapes, counterpointed by the pleasingly bitter abrasion at the finish; 14% alcohol.

PORTUGAL

🍷 **8** LB7 Lisboa 2018   **£6.99**
Briary-brambly dark-chocolate barbecue red at an alluring price; gently spicy and grippy in the approved Portuguese manner; 13.5% alcohol. LB7, I gather, is the postcode of Lisbon's central district which may or may not be the bit of the city depicted on the jolly seaside-postcard-type label illustration.

🍷 **8** **Agenda Dão 2018**   **£7.99**
Clearly a crowd pleaser, marketed by Majestic as 'Manager's Choice Dão' in a vote by staff (Majestic employs 1,000). It's a softly savoury middleweight with gentle fruitcake spice amid the berry fruit and a decent grip; 13% alcohol.

RED WINES

10 The Guv'nor £6.99

Well dang me. I'd expected the worst of this gimmicky item, but The Guv'nor, labelled only with that description in typewriter face, rules OK: opaque in colour and correspondingly concentrated in juicy-plumptious darkly spicy and thoroughly Spanish savoury black fruits, it's warmly weighty and splendidly balanced for a wholesome finish; 14% alcohol. Made by La Mancha giant Felix Solis, presumably just for Majestic, it's a blend of Tempranillo and Garnacha of indeterminate locale or vintage, and at the mix-six price it's a gift. *Olé*!

8 Dardell Organic Garnacha Tinta Syrah 2020 £8.99

Reassuringly deep beetroot colour and a dark savoury-spicy nose denote the gripping black fruits in this Catalan 80/20 Garnacha-Syrah blend from organic vines. Best bit is the attack of the keen blackberry fruit, which broadens out into middleweight heft and a brisk finish; 14% alcohol.

9 Bardos Roble Ribera del Duero 2018 £9.99

Ooh. A lovely sinewy-minty-spicy pure Tempranillo from the enigmatic Ribera del Duero region by excellent Bodegas de Bardos. Spiky but rich black-fruit flavours sleeked by four months in French oak *(roble)* casks; 14% alcohol. Incomprehensible arty and thoroughly Spanish scene of desolation on the sparse label further deepens the mystery of its high-country origin. Good value for this on-trend zone, reduced on mix six from £12.99.

SPAIN

RED WINES

SPAIN

🍷 7 **Viña Alarde Rioja Gran Reserva 2013** £9.99

It's actually rather slight, faded probably, from age. My Gran would certainly have had her reservations about it. The fruit is sweetly ripe and the vanilla all over it, but it does have a certain decrepit charm and at the mix-six price it's just about a deal; 13.5% alcohol.

PINK WINES

FRANCE

🍷 8 **Mon Plaisir du Sud Rosé 2020** £6.99

Pale salmon-pink Grenache-based Languedoc rosé exclusive to Majestic with a sweet strawberry nose but notably crisp'n'dry style to its fulsome fruit flavours; 12.5% alcohol. Good value, especially compared to many much-pricier rivals from neighbouring Provence.

WHITE WINES

ENGLAND

🍷 8 **Three Choirs Stone Brook 2020** £9.99

From a longstanding and versatile winery in Gloucestershire, an attractive dry wine with allusions of sweet red-apple on the nose and in the mouth, very wholesome and fresh, distantly evoking proper West Country farm cider while every inch a wine. You might think of a kind of mineral but low-acid Sauvignon but the constituent grapes are the perplexingly unfamiliar Siegerebbe, Solaris and Phoenix; hard to describe, easy to drink and to enjoy; 11% alcohol. It's rather expensive at £11.99 list, but I am happy loyally to sing its praises.

WHITE WINES

FRANCE

10 **Definition Sauternes 2010 37.5cl** £9.99
If you like Sauternes, you'll love this. It's pure gold in colour, wildly perfumed, honeyed, ambrosial and balanced and possibly from a great estate of the appellation. OK 2010 is a so-so vintage, but there's botrytis here and the wine is already drinking beautifully; 13% alcohol. It's madly underpriced. Try it and if you're convinced, invest.

9 **Kuhlmann-Platz Riesling Cuvée Prestige 2020** £10.99
Exotic minerally Alsace wine by Hunawhir co-operative, bracing and racy and brimming with aromatic-spicy white orchard and citrus fruits; a classic of its kind, a great harbinger for the 2020 harvest in Alsace and good value for this sort of quality; 12.5% alcohol.

9 **Castelnau de Suduiraut 2013 37.5cl** £12.99
Second wine of a grand Sauternes estate on terrific form in this well-thought-of stickie-Bordeaux vintage is glowing gold in colour, honeyed with orange-blossom allusions on the nose and beautifully balanced. Ambrosial is not overstating it; 13.5% alcohol.

WHITE WINES

GERMANY

10 Dr Hermann Ürziger Würzgarten
Riesling Auslese 2005   **£14.99**

Glorious moselle from one of the greatest vintages of the present century in its prime at this age: limpid gold colour, pure sweet-apple perfume with remote suggestions of honeysuckle, racy golden minerally Riesling fruit carrying the faint 'petrolly' mark of maturity, not sweet but lush and rich balanced by sublime slaty citrus acidity; just 8% alcohol. A perfect example of arguably the world's best wine style at a very keen mix-six price. A wistful reminder of the old days, when Majestic director of 40 years Tony Mason (who died in 2021) used to visit his German winemaker chums regularly in search of parcels of old and great wines to offer his adoring customers back in Blighty.

GREECE

8 Lyrarakis Assyrtiko 2020   **£9.99**

It's from Crete and genuinely evokes the joys of Greek-island leisure. The gentle Aegean tide is metaphorised in the very faint petillance of the wine, its delicately saline flavours full of sun, citrus and refreshment; it's dry but aromatic, wistful in its subtle fruitfulness; 13% alcohol. Well all right, I'm overdoing it – pining after Greece probably – but it's a proper summer wine to prompt sunny notions and very handsomely presented.

WHITE WINES

ITALY

🍷 8 **Nero Oro Grillo Appassimento 2019**   £7.49

Sicily's indigenous Grillo grape, once consigned ignominiously to the production of sticky Marsala, has caught on of late as a characterful fresh dry white. Here's a variation made with added must from dried, concentrated grapes for a fuller, richer style. Sweet-apple aroma is taken up by layered orchard fruit flavours with notes of sherry, marzipan and honey, lifted by lemon twang; good heft, 13.5% alcohol, rich rather than sweet. An interesting aperitif or match for poultry as well as fishy dishes.

SOUTH AFRICA

🍷 8 **Definition Chenin Blanc 2020**   £9.99

Comfortably plush aperitif wine, it has the expected Cape Chenin characteristics of honeyed perfume and peach-sweet-pear and nectarine ripeness counterpointed by crafty citrus acidity; 14% alcohol.

🍷 8 **Gabb Family Chardonnay 2020**   £9.99

Another plush vintage for this Stellenbosch stalwart with peachy-pineapple ripeness (13.5% alcohol) at ease with the creamy oak influence and balanced by limey acidity; the mix-six price I paid was a one-third reduction from the ambitious £14.99 single-bottle tag.

SPAIN

🍷 8 **The Guv'nor Vino Blanco**   £6.99

This mystery dry white made for Majestic by La Mancha producer Felix Solis is aromatic and assertive; strong minty-tropical savours will make it a versatile food match and there's a long finish; 12.5% alcohol. No vintage declared, but Majestic admits to a blend of Verdejo, Chardonnay and Sauvignon Blanc. In terms of style, it just about makes sense.

WHITE WINES

9   **Dardell Garnacha Blanca Viognier 2019**   **£8.99**
Much emphasis on the organic standing of this Catalan wine, made on a Tarragona estate that's been in the family of current owner Pepe Fuster for 'many generations'. Well, it's a wine with old-fashioned virtues: big lemon-gold colour, lively citrus-nectarine perfume, lots of heft (13.5% alcohol), leaving lingering glycerine legs up the sides of the glass and grabby pleasingly saline resiny white fruit flavours. Much to say about this wine and much to enjoy, even if a wee bit pricy at £10.99 list.

——Marks & Spencer——

For all their troubles, M&S do at least continue to add to their wine range at something approaching the rate at which they are deleting so many of my old favourites. Mustn't grumble, I suppose.

Succeeding 2020's introductions of the appealing 'Classics' and boring budget 'This is' ranges, they've followed up in 2021 with a new collection of 'Found' wines – intimating that M&S's intrepid wine buying/making teams have been scouring the world's vineyards for as-yet undiscovered gems. Some of the wines, possibly not all, are also available for home delivery from M&S's new partner Ocado as well as from M&S's own wine website.

I particularly mention online, because my forays this year into stores have yielded rather disappointing numbers of interesting wines actually on the shelves. Really big M&S food stores are presumably a better bet than the bucolic branches I've been haunting.

I like the 'Found' wines, and discover, now that I've counted up, that eight of the 30-odd bottles I've described this year are from the range. They look good with their cool vintage-photograph labels and hail from interesting places of varying remoteness including highland Greece, the Pyrenees and somewhere in the Andes. More significantly, the wines I have tried have been consistently delicious in their own ways and approachably priced, all at under £10.

RED WINES

ARGENTINA

8 Las Dalias Malbec 2020   £9.00

Unusually for a Mendoza Malbec in this price range it's made without oak ageing, and all the better for it, say I: big (14% alcohol) but juicy blackberry flavours with easy grip and a lick of mint chocolate; stands out, and I like the name 'The Dahlias' amid the blooms on the label.

8 Found Cabernet Franc 2019   £10.00

I went for this because it's made by Catena, one of the great names of Mendoza, and it's not Malbec. Cabernet Franc is a minority blending grape of Bordeaux and also a mainstay of red Loire wines, but here it has been fashioned into a fascinatingly rich and pruny-brambly red-meat wine of satisfying robustness; it's smoothed from oak contact but vivid and juicy; 13.5% alcohol. I like the tango dancers on the label.

AUSTRALIA

8 Burra Brook Cabernet Sauvignon 2020   £7.00

Stalwart SE Australia claret-style Cabernet (not so much 'upfront' as harmonious and balanced) has a native eucalyptus note to the darkly ripe cassis fruit, smoothed with some oak-contact wine in the blend; 14% alcohol. M&S suggest pairing this with sausages and mash. Sage advice.

RED WINES

**8 Langhorne Creek Cabernet
    Sauvignon 2020**   £7.00
South Australia's vineyards were hit hard in 2020 by
weather and wildfires but it was frost in September 2019
that particularly ravaged Langhorne Creek's vintage.
Some farms lost half their crop, but the fruit quality
at harvest has been reported as exceptional. This all-
Cabernet barbecue red stakes the claim: proper cassis
juiciness in the intense black-fruit flavours, balanced and
wholesome, 14.5% alcohol, and good value.

8 Lock Keeper's Reserve Shiraz 2020   £9.00
Murray River blend with Petit Verdot and (white grape)
Colombard marked out by an easy weight, juicy red berry
fruits and cushiony plumpness; artlessly likeable; 13.5%
alcohol. I picked it up for just £6 on promo.

8 M&S Classics No. 11 Corbières 2019   £8.00
Substantial Mediterranean garrigue-spiced blackberry-
barbed winter red with intensity and grip; 13.5% alcohol.
Definitely the better kind of Corbières. If the 2020
replaces, risk it.

8 Lirac Les Closiers 2019   £10.00
Silky and really quite substantial but unoaked Rhône
red from a village *cru* which is perpetually compared for
quality and style with Châteauneuf du Pape, no less. This
is intense with darkly ripe berry fruits, savoury spice and
lingering juiciness; 14% alcohol. M&S commend this as
a match for spicy sausages. Hear hear!

AUSTRALIA

FRANCE

RED WINES

FRANCE

9 M&S Classics No. 36 Bourgogne Pinot Noir 2018 £12.00

This was my top pick from the new 'Classics' range launched by M&S in 2020 and it was still available at press time in 2021. Healthy, earthy Pinot in authentic regional style probably with some oak contact contributing to its juicy raspberry sleekness; 13% alcohol. The 2019 vintage, if it follows, should be a safe bet.

GREECE

9 Found Xinomavro-Mandilaria 2019 £9.50

Most of us wouldn't, I'd guess, pluck this from the shelf on the off chance. The weird name, puzzling fishing-boat photo and obscure origin must surely cast all but the most intrepid wine shopper adrift. But this is from M&S's new 'Found' range. It's supposed to be serendipitous. And reader, it's worth the punt. Xinomavro and Mandilaria are the grape varieties employed, the boat is possibly a metaphor for the Aegean and the origin is Naoussa in the far north of mainland Greece, far from the sea but rated the nation's number one quality wine region. And this wine's a cracker, juicy, poised and grippy with ripe lush black fruits; it's of its own style but experts compare Xinomavro to the fabled wines of Barolo and this one shows you why; 13.5% alcohol.

ITALY

9 Classics No 23 Chianti Riserva 2017 £8.00

I missed this among my little collection from M&S's Classics launch last year and am glad to have caught up with it. Authentic Chianti style partnering plump cherry-raspberry fruit with a bit of vanilla (riserva wines are kept a year in oak) and convincingly firm tannin to complete, it's wholesome and natural-tasting; 13.5% alcohol.

Marks & Spencer

RED WINES

ITALY

🍷 **8** **La Cascata Passivento 2019** £9.00

The craze for *appassimento* wines has spread decisively from Verona, where Valpolicella has been getting fortified with concentrated-grape must for ever, to the southerly climes of Puglia, home to grapes Primitivo and Negroamaro which lend themselves happily to the treatment. This one's great after you get over the unnerving nomenclature that seems to say 'passing wind'. It's properly dark and soupy even though unoaked and newly bottled, with sweet spices and dried fruits, smooth abrasion of ripe hedgerow fruits and 14% alcohol. Meaty dishes, pungent cheeses, cold nights.

SPAIN

🍷 **9** **El Duque de Miralta Reserva Rioja 2015** £12.00

New vintage – and the best-rated year for Rioja since 2010 – for this recently introduced new series made for M&S by serious bodega El Coto, this is sweetly oaked, maturing but bright with cherry-cassis fruit, enigmatically aromatic and ideally balanced; easy weight and 13.5% alcohol. It's not cheap, but it's worth it.

PINK WINES

FRANCE

🍷 **8** **Cintu Île de Beauté Rosé 2020** £10.00

You've got to give credit to M&S for diversity – and not just the new 'Found' range of wines from unexpected places. This 'Winemaker's Selection' Corsican pink is artily bottled in clear glass (I can remember when all M&S rosé was bottled in green to preserve the delicate colours) showing off the pale copper/onion-skin hue and revealing a really distinctive citrus-peach twang, very dry and fresh; 11.5% alcohol. It's from indigenous Corsican varieties Sciacarellu and Niellucciu. Just so you know.

PORTUGAL

PINK WINES

8 Found Rosé Vinho Verde 2020   £7.00

If pink vinho verde seems an aberration, be reminded that at home in the Minho Valley of northwest Portugal vinho verde was originally a red wine; the white version is a recent confection devised for the export market. Cheerful pink hue, floral soft-red-fruit scent and a detectable spritz make this confection forgivably agreeable. It's vinho verde made rosé by the addition of a large measure (two-thirds) of red wine from Touriga Nacional, the great grape of Port production, and it works surprisingly well; fruity (soft pear, strawberry) short of sweet, fresh and lively; 11% alcohol.

WHITE WINES

**8 Tierra Y Hombre Casablanca
Sauvignon Blanc 2020**   £7.00

Very glad to see this consistent bargain has survived all the changes and deletions at M&S. It has a bracing tang at the outset, lots of asparagus-gooseberry savour in the mouth and a nifty lemon lift; 12.5% alcohol. Nice smoked-salmon match.

CHILE

8 Classics No 26 Sauvignon Blanc 2020   £8.00

Casablanca Valley wine is, I suppose, a classic of the Chilean Sauvignon kind, but arguably better than that because it has more keen definition of fruit than many I can think of and a proper racy-grassy lushness to the exotic ripe flavours referencing pineapple and nectarine among others; 13.5% alcohol.

WHITE WINES

FRANCE

9 **Found Gros Manseng 2020** £9.00

From Gascony in the mysterious southwest of France and made entirely from equally enigmatic Gros Manseng grapes, this is a good choice for M&S's new 'Found' range. And it's great: aromatic, limpid dry white with peachy richness and a fleeting cinnamon note but keen, refreshing and balanced; 12.5% alcohol. This is a relatively new style of Gros Manseng wine – the grapes used to be reserved for the lush late-harvested sweet wines of Jurançon.

8 **Chablis Cave des Vignerons 2019** £12.00

Nice whiff of struck match on this authentically delicious new vintage of a wine made by M&S with Chablis's Cave des Vignerons co-op for more than 25 years – during which time, I am pleased to assert, the label design seems to have changed not one whit. It's reliably ripe, balanced and typical and if not cheap, a fair deal; 12.5% alcohol.

GERMANY

9 **M&S Classics No 2 Mineralstein Riesling 2019** £9.50

Launched in 2020 as one of the stars of the new 'Classics' range, a spiffing hock by former M&S full-timer Gerd Stepp from his ancestral vineyards in the Rheinpfalz. You get a big whack of crisp apple fruit, ripe but zingy, fresh but lengthy in savour, full rather in the Alsace Riesling style and 12% alcohol. This is a food wine and one that will develop in the bottle. M&S's own note advises it will keep fruitfully for up to five years.

WHITE WINES

GREECE

8 **Found Moschofilero-Roditis 2020** £8.50
If you're new to the wines of the Peloponnese, the extensive semi-detached southwestern region of mainland Greece, give this one a shot. It's dry but delightfully aromatic, grapey and nectary in ripeness but tangy-briny in its breezy freshness; 12% alcohol. A genuine discovery from M&S new 'Found' range.

9 **Soave 2020** £5.00
At the price, a quite remarkably decent example of this once-fashionable Verona dry white, very dry and pleasantly green-tasting with a little lick of white-nut alongside the trademark citrus twang; 11.5% alcohol. Nice partner to creamy pasta as well as fishy dishes.

ITALY

8 **Orvieto 2020** £6.00
Orvieto is a pre-Roman hilltown (the name comes from Latin *urbs vetus*, old city) of Umbria once famous for its delicately aromatic white wines, now rather forgotten. So it's pleasant to recall the still-distinctive pear-blossom and lemon aromas and savours of this welcome revival; 12% alcohol. Nicely made and jolly cheap.

8 **Found Ribolla Gialla 2020** £7.00
Label featuring a vintage photo of an old Fiat 500 puffing up a steep cobbled hilltown street drew me to this enigmatic dry Friuli white from the new 'Found' range. Ribolla Gialla is the grape variety, local to the Dolomite foothills of Friuli-Venezia-Giulia and gives good colour, spicy aroma and crisp brightness to the fresh white fruits; 12% alcohol.

WHITE WINES

ITALY

🍷 8 **Garganega Pinot Grigio 2019** £7.00
Rather striking IGT blend joins Garganega, the grape of
Soave and ever-popular PG to make an impressively crisp
cabbage-citrus style evocative of Soave, blanched-almond
richness included, of real interest; 12.5% alcohol.

NEW ZEALAND

🍷 9 **Saint Clair James Sinclair Sauvignon**
Blanc 2020 £15.00
I was looking forward to trying this follow-up to the
excellent 2019 vintage, featured here last time round, and
it's come well up to snuff. The 2020 vintage is reckoned
exceptional in New Zealand and this has a particular
ripeness and complexity of fruit. There are the expected
asparagus and gooseberry notes on nose and palate but
here too, I kid you not, is more than a suggestion of Kiwi
fruit. How apt is that? Very good indeed, which it needs
to be at the price; 13% alcohol.

SOUTH AFRICA

🍷 8 **Fresh & Fruity Chenin Blanc 2020** £5.00
From M&S's new (well, 2020) budget range, a very
decent Cape dry aperitif wine with crisp impact and
artfully contrasting honeysuckle aromatics; it has good
heft (13% alcohol) and convincing balance.

🍷 9 **Found Grenache Blanc 2020** £8.00
The Grenache Blanc grape has only quite recently found
recognition in its indigenous setting, southwest France,
and here it is already getting the M&S imprimatur in
southwest South Africa. Fair enough, I say, as this is
comparable even to its best Rhône counterparts. You get
fine yellow colour, ripe sweet-melon perfume with a nice
cabbagey crispness and a big whack of luscious even rich
orchard and hothouse white fruits; 14% alcohol. Price is
fair and you get ostriches on the label.

SPARKLING WINES

FRANCE

9 **Found Blanquette de Limoux**   £10.00

Languedoc wine from the new 'Found' range is a discovery indeed. It's a lively full-fizz sparkler made by the 'traditional' (champagne) method and delivers vivid crisp orchard-fruit flavours with a little bit of honeyed ripeness and a citrus twang besides; 12% alcohol. Really good and good value too.

SPAIN

8 **Prestige Cava Rosado**   £10.00

This featured in my live tasting of Valentine's Day pink fizzes on Channel 4's *Sunday Brunch*, and it went down well. Everyone admired the full colour, persistent sparkle and involving strawberry-raspberry fruit ripeness to the crisp flavours; 11% alcohol. It's made at the Segura Viudas winery, owned by cava giant Freixenet.

Morrisons

It's not been a vintage year for Morrisons. Profits halved between 2020 and 2021 thanks to the pandemic, and the business even lost its prestigious place on the London Stock Exchange Top 100 companies.

As a publicly listed entity with reportedly undervalued shares, Morrisons became a target for takeover. In the summer of 2021, a bidding war broke out among a number of private equity companies – the hyenas of high-finance – anxious to seize the UK's fourth-largest supermarket at a price far lower than its true worth.

As this year's guide went to press, the board of Morrisons had just approved a £7,000,000,000 offer from an American bidder. The aspiring new owners gave assurances they had the best of intentions. Morrisons' customers (11 million each week, we are told), its 110,000 employees and countless suppliers will have to wait and see.

What a sad fate for this splendid family food business founded in Bradford, West Yorkshire, in 1899. From a simple market stall selling farm produce it grew first into a network of shops then into supermarkets in the 1960s. Operations were confined largely to northern England until as late as 2004 before the company, under the leadership of Ken Morrison, suddenly took over Safeway and went nationwide.

Its rise has been meteoric, and the wine range has kept up with it all very convincingly. While at first I found the store displays bewildering, there's no doubting the breadth and depth of the quality and diversity of the range. Once you get acquainted with the Morrisons' wine department, it's a pleasure to cruise it.

As with the other supermarkets I have chosen this year's wines to try on the basis of following up on the best performers from previous vintages and making the occasional foray into less-familiar territory when I have come across new wines. Unsurprisingly, there have been only a few significant additions to the Morrisons list during the pandemic period.

When the names of wines in the following pages are prefixed 'The Best' they are from Morrisons' premium own-label range, usually indicated by a discreet neck label. Many of these are among the best buys, and are regularly available on generous discount. Look out, too, for occasional blanket promotions based on the well-tried and now industry-wide promotional formula of buy six or more bottles, get 25% off the lot.

RED WINES

ARGENTINA

 9 The Best Uco Valley Gran Montana Malbec 2020 £7.75

Morrisons' own team worked with top Mendoza winery Catena to make this crafty blend with Cabernet into a distinctly delicious blend of rich blackberry-pie savour with keen spicy edginess in lip-smacking balance; 14.5% alcohol. Made for beefy feasting.

AUSTRALIA

8 19 Crimes Red Wine 2020 £9.00

This wine and several others under the same brand are made by Australian giant Treasury Wine Estates. It is said to be the biggest-selling mass-market brand in Britain and you can buy wines from the range in just about every supermarket. I'm reviewing it here because I bought my bottle in Morrisons on promo for £7. Now here I must admit to a natural antipathy for global brands, so I approached this tasting without enthusiasm – and was confounded. The wine is healthy, well-made from Shiraz *et al* in the better Australian manner; defined, balanced, juicy and pleasantly long, by no means overweight or overripe; 13.5% alcohol. Any suspicions I had that all the investment has gone into the barmy marketing campaign for 19 Crimes, including telephone apps in which the characters on the labels come to life and speak, should not put you off. Next year, I'll try some more from the range and report further.

RED WINES

Morrisons (vertical, left margin)

FRANCE (vertical tab)

🍷 9 **Raoul Clerget Beaujolais** £5.00

No vintage date on my bottle but it's the match of the 2019 I rated highly last year, and still the same remarkable bargain at a fiver. Juicy-purple bouncing raspberry-bright refresher with 13% alcohol and a good attitude to being chilled awhile for maximum enjoyment.

🍷 9 **The Best Languedoc 2018** £7.75

This ripplingly textured garrigue winter red of impressive power (13.5% alcohol) and long savour is a dependable perennial benefitting from ten months in oak casks. From Narbonne-born winemaking legend and former French rugby international Gérard Bertrand.

🍷 8 **Cairanne Le Verdier Cru des Côtes du Rhône J. Boulard 2019** £10.00

Got this new vintage (yet another epic harvest in the region) for £8 and very pleased with it. It's muscular without being hard, dark in colour and intensity of spicy blackberry fruit with grippy texture and long savour; 14.5% alcohol. It might well repay keeping a year or two.

ITALY (vertical tab)

🍷 8 **Morrisons Organic Montepulciano D'Abruzzo 2019** £6.75

Nicely poised juicy cherry-redcurrant glugger with traces of mint chocolate and a limpid purity of flavour somehow in tune with its organic status; 12.5% alcohol. It is pleasingly typical of the DOC's style and a better wine than Morrisons' standard £5.00 non-organic Montepulciano. Bought on offer at just £5.50.

RED WINES

ITALY

🍷 8 **The Best Nerello Mascalese 2019** £7.75
Strapping blueberry-pruny indigenous red from Sicily
is as distinctive in its spicy savour as it is in jazzy
packaging – definitely one to look out for in Morrisons'
regular promos, down to an unnecessarily diminished £6.
Briskly gripping in its finish, it's big (13.5% alcohol), so a
good match for meaty dishes as well as sticky pasta, and
might well develop in bottle if given half a chance.

🍷 9 **The Best Toscana 2018** £9.00
A Morrisons one-off made specially by San Felice,
a very proper Chianti Classico estate, combining
Chianti's backbone grape Sangiovese with Cabernet
Sauvignon, Merlot and other non-indigenous varieties
into a 'supertuscan blend of luscious, intense and
thoroughly Tuscan character'. And succeeding very
well in the enterprise, as far as I'm concerned. Terrific
stuff and good value; 12.5% alcohol.

SPAIN

🍷 8 **Carta Roja Tempranillo 2020** £7.00
La Mancha everyday red of vigorous and throughly
Spanish character has full fruit in spite of relative youth
and modest woof (12% alcohol); particularly good value
on occasional 2-for-£10 promo.

🍷 8 **The Best Marques de Los Rios**
Rioja Reserva 2016 £8.75
Down in price from last year's £10 for the decent 2014,
this has strawberry-sweet ripeness and a bit of creamy
vanilla all in easy balance; 13% alcohol.

Morrisons

RED WINES

SPAIN

🍷 9 **The Best Priorat 2016**   £10.00

Of this 2016 I wrote in last year's *Best Wines* 'This is the same vintage I raved about last year. Why on earth hasn't it sold out?' Well, I'm here to tell you it still hasn't done so. I bought my bottle in late spring 2021 at £8 on promo and if anything it's even more of a treat than it was in 2020 or 2019. To reiterate, it's an authentic pungent-silky easy-weighted licorice-chocolate and plummy black-fruit exotic, oaked and rich red from a cult region growing into its maturity; 14.5% alcohol. I think it might be the typographically challenging label that's inhibiting sales. Take full advantage: this is a true bargain.

WHITE WINES

CHILE

🍷 8 **Cono Sur Bicicleta Viognier 2020**   £7.50

I do hate the annoying cycling-theme labels on this really good series of varietals (I've liked earlier vintages of the full-flavoured Sauvignon Blanc). Cono Sur vineyard workers, we gather, cycle about their duties rather than travelling in motorised vehicles, thus saving the planet. But pay no heed to this virtue-signalling: this is a fine exotic dry wine with hallmark apricot-mango ripeness and tangy citrus lift all in happy harmony; 13% alcohol.

FRANCE

🍷 9 **Pomerols Picpoul de Pinet 2020**   £8.00

An alluring hedgerow-blossom whiff accompanies the seabreeze twang on the nose of this sharp new vintage from the excellent Pomerols co-op, a leading Picpoul producer. The crisp fruit is full and eager with a signature saline note and 13% alcohol. It's been on promo at £6.50 and is a great partner to oysters, mussels and fish stews and soups.

WHITE WINES

🍷 8 The Best Alsace Pinot Gris 2019   £8.50

Alsace had a particularly fortuitous vintage in 2019, and this lavishly coloured, exotically aromatic, plumply ripe, smoky-spicy PG gives a clear clue – lusciously good but liftingly bright aperitif wine of proper Alsace character; 13% alcohol. It's by prolific co-op Cave de Turckheim, on good form, and has been on promo at £7.50.

🍷 9 The Best Vouvray 2019   £8.75

Seductive Chenin Blanc from a famed appellation on the north bank of the Loire near Tours. It blooms with honeysuckle scent but is only just off-dry, peachy and plump with vivid citrus outside flavours, exotic and delightful; 12.5% alcohol. Classy aperitif and a match for all sorts of white and cured meats as well as fish and blue cheese. I paid £7 on promo.

🍷 9 The Best Chablis 2019   £13.00

Lavish green-gold colour, marked gunflint/struck-match mineral aroma at the front of the nose and thrilling classic Chablis Chardonnay fruit – pure and river-fresh with lifting citrus twang – of real character; 12.5% alcohol. For a basic AC Chablis £13 looks expensive (I paid £11 on promo, mind you) but this is worth it – and a better buy than this year's Morrisons' Best Chablis 1er Cru 2018 (£15).

🍷 9 Morrisons Soave 2020   £4.25

Plain-wrapper house wine that is startlingly good for the money, fresh and typical of the Soave style with gently green aromas and fruit and a little nutty lushness besides; 11.5% alcohol.

Morrisons

WHITE WINES

ITALY

🍷 9 **The Best Soave Classico 2019** £6.50
Enticing Veronese classic with attractive green-shot-with-pale-gold colour, vivid stored-apple aroma and crisp matching fruit hinting at citrus twang and a blanched-almond lick; lovely balance and brisk finish; 12% alcohol. Good price and a bargain at the £5.50 I paid on promo.

🍷 8 **The Best Gavi 2020** £8.00
Dependable Piedmont dry wine by dependable Piedmont scale producer Araldica; brisk and pleasingly vegetal in this new vintage; 12.5% alcohol.

🍷 10 **Minea Greco di Tufo 2018** £8.75
I'm top-scoring it because I picked it up in July 2021 on promo for £5.50 – one of the true bargains of the year. If the offer is repeated on this or on any subsequent vintage, don't miss it. Greco's the grape and Tufo the village in the Campania where the vines have flourished in the volcanic soil since first planted by Greek settlers thousands of years back. Well, so the story goes. The wine is handsomely coloured, headily perfumed and at once rich in aromatic white fruit and cleanly crisp with a distinct orange-grapefruit acidity; 12.5% alcohol.

NEW ZEALAND

🍷 9 **The Best Marlborough Sauvignon Blanc 2020** £8.00
I'm sticking to my guns and reiterating my note on the 2019 to say this one also evokes mangetout among the references for its aromas and savours – along with the customary green pepper, asparagus and gooseberry. Actually I liked it even better than last year's for its focus, joyfulness and sheer zing; 13% alcohol. Made by admirable Yealands estate in the Awatere.

WHITE WINES

NEW ZEALAND

9 Mastercraft Single Vineyard Sauvignon Blanc 2020   £10.00

Generic Kiwi Sauvignon is losing its cachet, but here's a wine from an individual (if unnamed) vineyard in Marlborough's Wairau to remind us of the excitement these wines once generated. It's thrillingly zingy with grassy-gooseberry-green-pepper aromas and flavours, truly refreshing and bright, and heftily ripe (13.5% alcohol) into the bargain. And talking of bargains, I got two bottles of this at Morrisons on promo for £12.00 in the spring of 2021.

SOUTH AFRICA

8 Klein Street Chardonnay 2020   £6.50

I've been a fan of Klein Street, a producer in the Cape Town region, since discovering their fabulous Grenache Blanc at Morrisons in 2018. Morrisons promptly dropped it. Happens all the time. Boo. But here's a fresh start: the Chardonnay is perky-crisp but fleetingly plush with exotic fruit notes, balanced and twangy; 12.5% alcohol. It's good value, and has been promoted this year at £10 for two bottles. That's cheap.

8 The Best South African Sauvignon Blanc 2020   £6.75

Grassy texture to the fruit of this fresh Stellenbosch bargain (I paid £5 on promo) reveals a likeable grapefruit twang to the satisfyingly ripe fruit medley; 12.5% alcohol.

8 The Best Bush Vine Chenin Blanc 2020   £8.25

Nicely contrived balancing act from Swartland demonstrating the distinctive qualities of Cape Chenin Blanc: bright crisp freshness lit by citrussy acidity alongside honeysuckle-scented ripe apple and tropical fruits; 12.5% alcohol. Got this for £6 on promo.

WHITE WINES

8 **The Best Marques de Los Riojas**
Rioja Blanco 2020 £7.75

Modern-day citrussy dry Rioja makes a nod to the old days with a little vanilla lick from oak contact amid the melon and orchard fruit freshness; 13% alcohol. It is unconnected with the fabled reserva under the same brand name one-removed below, made by a different bodega.

8 **The Best Fervenza Albariño 2019** £8.25

Muscadet-like green-fruit briny seaside-fresh food white (shellfish, charcuterie) from Atlantic Spain is assertively tangy and crisp; 12% alcohol. Look out for the 'aromas of orange peel'.

10 **The Best Marques de Los Rios**
Rioja Blanco Reserva 2016 £13.00

Luscious creamy old-fashioned oak-matured dry white Rioja by excellent Baron de Ley bodega, as rich in exotic fruits as it is in gold-green colour; sweet melon and pineapple aromas are followed up faithfully on the palate and lifted by perfectly judged acidity; 12% alcohol. This extraordinary wine should be snapped up by Rioja lovers pining for the oxidative whites of the good old days, and equally by novices in search of true classic flavours. Morrisons occasionally reduce it to £11.

FORTIFIED WINES

PORTUGAL

9 **Morrisons 10-Year-Old Tawny Port** £12.00

Silky wood-aged port amply illustrates the merits of a long slumber in oak. This is just turning from the natural ruby colour of the new wine to the amber hue born of time spent in oxidative conditions of the kind that prevail inside casks, and very alluring it looks. The nose is sweet, spirity and promising and the fruit bright, figgy-nutty and seductively clingy. Did you know that sales of port in the UK rose by more than 10 per cent in 2020–2021? It's luscious, good-value old tawnies like this, from the Symington family, that I hope are leading the way.

SPARKLING WINES

ENGLAND

9 **Balfour Hush Heath 1503 Brut Rosé** £19.00

This 'extra dry' Kentish sparkler received universal approval in my nerve-wracking live appearance on Channel 4's *Sunday Brunch* programme on Valentine's Day 2021. What the presenters and celebrities didn't know was that I had not tasted it before. I chose it simply on the basis that its white stablemate (sold by the Co-op) is outstandingly good (see Co-op section). This came close: alluring coral colour, very busy mousse, alpine-strawberry bloom, soft red fruit flavours bright with crisp tang, fresh and long; distinctively delicious; 12% alcohol.

Sainsbury's

As is to be expected, most of my recommendations this year are from Sainsbury's formidable Taste the Difference (TTD) range. Sainsbury's started the whole supermarket-own-label thing back in the 1980s, just when I was first writing about wine in general and supermarket wine in particular, and there's a case for saying that they have been in pole position in this respect ever since.

But during the pandemic (and before), there has been attrition. Old friends have fallen by the wayside. In the last year, TTD Barbaresco, formerly described in these pages as 'slinky, gently gripping' and awarded maximum points, has disappeared. Italian distant neighbour TTD Greco di Tufo ('aromas and flavours evoking everything from apple to apricot, from fennel to sage') has also bitten the volcanic dust. Domaine du Colombier, the superb small-estate Chinon Sainsbury's espoused for a generation, was lately snuffed out. The in-house sherry range, a wonder of the world, has also evaporated.

I won't go on and on, but I could. Let's put these losses down to necessary retrenchment in these tragic times, and look forward.

All the wines featured here are bottles I have bought and tasted at home. As a now-seasoned personal shopper, I am proud to report that every one of them was purchased during the numerous 25%-off-six-or-more offers prevailing in 2021. These very welcome events seem to be growing in frequency, and they have saved me a fortune, especially when the blanket discount is superimposed on individual-promo lines. Here and there in the notes I have been unable to resist gloating over my little shopping triumphs.

Mind you, I wonder whether Sainsbury's aren't painting themselves into a corner with all this discounting. Will seasoned customers (the best kind, surely) get out of the habit of paying full price for wine?

Or is the whole thing a con? Is the true value of each wine the 25%-off price? I must say I don't believe so. Tracking supermarket prices for 20 years, as I have in this series of guides, Sainsbury's wines, and the TTD wines in particular, have shown remarkably little inflation, even in the light of steadily growing excise duty impositions. Maybe Brexit will, in time, hike the cost of wines from the Continent, but I'm not holding my breath.

RED WINES

ARGENTINA

9 Taste the Difference Morador Fairtrade Malbec 2019 £8.50

I admire the utilitarian determinism of the label design but am not convinced it does justice to the wine. You get big baked-fruit flavours from the off, sinewy and dark but not 'cooked' and an obvious match for spicy-meaty dishes along the lines of chilli con carne, of fond memory. Nice worthy wine, not cheap, but a fair trade indeed; 13.5% alcohol

AUSTRALIA

9 Taste the Difference Langhorne Creek Cabernet Sauvignon 2019 £7.50

Very consistent cool-climate (well, relatively) wine from South Australia about 50 miles from Adelaide where Cabernet has been the speciality for generations. Opaque ruby, sweet cassis honk and big classic-Cabernet purity of fruit is very trim in balance; 14.5% alcohol. Class act for the money, especially at the £6.50 I paid on promo.

FRANCE

9 Taste the Difference Languedoc 2019 £7.50

Middling in weight this year but brimming with lavish black-fruit flavours, spicy and gripping, this is as artful as ever, a generic Mediterranean wine every bit as beguiling as village-AC-rated counterparts priced very much higher; 13.5% alcohol. Frequently discounted, I got mine for under a fiver on promo.

Sainsbury's

FRANCE

RED WINES

🍷 8 Taste the Difference Beaujolais
Supérieur 2019   £8.00

This firm but juicily bouncy big-flavoured food wine from Mommesin is a step up from your everyday Beaujolais and worth the money (even compared to jolly £5 supermarket bottles); 13% alcohol. Beaujolais Supérieur is an official, if rarely seen, quality designation above Beaujolais AC and below Beaujolais Villages. So there.

🍷 9 Paul Jaboulet Aîné Côtes du Rhône
Villages Plan de Dieu 2018   £9.00

I found this in a mid-size store in early 2021 reduced to £6 and grabbed it, aware that Jaboulet is one of the great names of the Rhône Valley. The wine didn't disappoint: pitchy crimson colour, pungent sweet-spice nose, big whack of black fruit and an emphatic grip of conclusive tannin; 14% alcohol. The vineyards of the Plan de Dieu, as the back-label of this wine pointedly explains, lie between the two prestigious AC villages of Cairanne and Gigondas. The campaign similarly to elevate Plan de Dieu is no doubt under way.

🍷 8 Taste the Difference St Chinian 2018   £9.00

Deep, deep purple high-country Languedoc-wilderness wine with fruits-of-the-forest savours besides the garrigue spice, this is a decidedly determinist game red (venison/wild boar spring to mind) for chilly-winter feasts; genuinely of its place and deeply satisfying; 14.5% alcohol.

RED WINES

FRANCE

🍷 10 Taste the Difference Pic St Loup
Reserve 2018   £10.00

Long-awaited (by me anyway) 2018 vintage of this consistent favourite is a palpable hit. Already more ripely rounded (13.5% alcohol) than the tough 2017 was, it's creamy with oak contact, warmly spicy and briary and evocative of the garrigue country of the Languedoc in which the Pic St Loup, a stark mini-mountain of the Massif Centrale, is a prominent landmark. The wines have had their own appellation protegée only since 2017 and most have consequently risen in price, but this one is modestly down from the £11 asked for the 2017, and I got it for £7.50 on promo. Deal!

🍷 8 Cru des Côtes du Rhône Vinsobres 2018   £10.00

Handsome spicy dark wine of easy friendliness by cryptically named Vignerons de l'Enclave co-operative; rich but clearly defined in the right licorice-pungent manner in this fine vintage; 14.5% alcohol.

🍷 8 Fleurie Georges Duboeuf 2020   £10.00

You could say this is a bit of a rush job, as top *cru* Beaujolais tends to reach the market rather later than the ordinary ACs. Got it on a 25% off for six promo and at £7.50 we're talking a deal. But here's the thing. 'Good Fleurie ages quite well', says Wine Society Beaujolais buyer Tim Sykes, 'but few producers make the effort to make serious wine'. Well, this one isn't serious wine: I liked the youthful raspiness both of fruit and abrasion and it's brightly juicy, but I see no ageing potential. Good villages Beaujolais at best, and at the price I paid, it would be churlish to sniff too loudly.

RED WINES

FRANCE

🍷 9 **Taste the Difference Château
Bouysses Cahors Malbec 2017**   **£13.00**

Heroic single-estate wine from Cahors in the Lot Valley, it's a particularly succulent rendering of the Malbec grape, full of dark and concentrated blackberry savour, smoothed with oak contact and spiced with baked herbaceous tinges; 13% alcohol. The Malbec, once widely planted further north in Bordeaux but now the mainstay of Argentina's Andean vineyards, makes a very different style of wine at home in Cahors, and this one sets a very good example.

🍷 9 **Taste the Difference Salento
Primitivo 2019**   **£7.00**

ITALY

Ripe, sinewy, dark and satisfying IGT wine from Salento, the stacked heel of Italy's peninsular boot and southern extremity of the province of Puglia. The Primitivo grape, so known because it's the first variety to bud, flower, set fruit and ripen, here makes a lovely round but grippy food red to match the meatiest menus and spiciest pasta sauces; 13.5% alcohol. Forever being gratuitously discounted to £6, in which case a 10 score.

🍷 7 **Taste the Difference Chianti
Classico 2019**   **£9.00**

Straightforward cherry-berry sweetly ripe modern natural-tasting wine of charm rather than distinction, trim finish; 13.5% alcohol. Expensive for what it is.

RED WINES

ITALY

🍷 8 Taste the Difference Maremma Toscana 2019 £10.00

Maremma, a western coastal sub-region of Tuscany, has been recognised as a quality-wine DOC only since 2011 but is gathering steam. Red wines are typically a blend of native Sangiovese (the grape of neighbouring Chianti) with Cabernet Sauvignon. This one's typical: black-cherry-violet aromas, plumpness of Cabernet cassis fruit with brightness of Sangiovese, not like Chianti but somehow Italian in a 'supertuscan' sort of way; a hefty crowd-pleaser tasting expensive and soothing; 14.5% alcohol.

NEW ZEALAND

🍷 10 Ara Select Blocks Pinot Noir 2020 £9.00

Wildly exuberant cherry-raspberry aroma from this pale but beautifully garnet-coloured Marlborough wine runs with complete continuity into the startlingly bright and piquant pure juicy Kiwi Pinot fruit. A style entirely of its own (forget burgundy) and a terrific match for tricky menus such as fish soup, salad niçoise or cold cuts as well as the traditional Pinot partners of white meats, poultry and game birds; 13% alcohol. I loved it and can't fault it at the unusally modest price. Consider cooling it for appropriate occasions.

PORTUGAL

🍷 8 Feuerheerd's Anchor Wine 2018 £11.00

New vintage for this surprise discovery of last year, a respectable Douro table wine in a zany gift-wrap kind of package. It's darkly opaque and distinctly porty (aged a year in old vintage-port casks) in aroma with rich black fruit and spice, altogether savoury and satisfying; 13.5% alcohol. Dietrich Feuerheerd was a Hamburg-born merchant who set up in Oporto in 1815 as a merchant and port shipper in the wake of Waterloo.

RED WINES

SOUTH AFRICA

🍷 8 **Bruce Jack Pinotage Malbec 2020**   £7.00
Most unusual blend of the Cape's native grape Pinotage with ubiquitous Malbec making a big cherry-bramble juicy glugger with a nice herbal twist, clean finish and plenty of woof at 14.5% alcohol.

🍷 8 **Sheep Hill Shiraz Malbec 2020**   £7.00
Another welcome addition to the burgeoning flock of wines now made worldwide with sheep on the label – perhaps inspired by the Mouton (actually 'little hill' in context, rather than sheep, but never mind) of Rothschild fame in Bordeaux. This humbler manifestation is very much in the Cape style: ripe (13.5% alcohol), summer-red-fruit juicy and highlighted by notes of warm spice and eucalyptus, nicely weighted and with gentle grip.

SPAIN

🍷 9 **Taste the Difference Navarra 2018**   £7.00
Still on shelf from last year and all the better for it, this robust Garnacha-based food red (sausage to sirloin) has mellow blackberry-blueberry depths with savour and grip; 13.5% alcohol. Navarra is neighbour to Rioja and consequently gets overlooked: a region deserving more attention.

🍷 8 **Taste the Difference Rioja Viñedos
Barrihuelo Crianza 2017**   £7.75
This maturing wine has more vanilla creaminess than you might expect from a briefly oak-aged crianza ('nursery') wine and lots of bright cassis fruit besides; left over from last year and turning out very well from the added bottle age; 13.5% alcohol.

RED WINES

SPAIN

🍷 **8** Taste the Difference Ribera del
Duero Roble 2018 £10.00

New to me, this Ribera del Duero is made by Rioja bodega CVNE and has appreciable blackcurrant concentration, sweet ripeness and plenty of grip with 14.5% alcohol. I'm sure it could do with more time in bottle to come round. Accordingly, the back label notes that 'this iconic region is renowned for producing a powerful style of red wine that ages well'. So hold on to it for a bit. Ignore the further note: 'It is recommended that this wine be consumed within one year of purchase'. Ho hum.

WHITE WINES

AUSTRALIA

🍷 **9** Taste the Difference Barossa
Riverland Chardonnay 2020 £7.00

Ripe peach and melon lushness with signature sweet-apple Chardonnay lift made plush with a bit of oak contact, this hardy perennial by leading Barossa estate Chateau Tanunda has an elegant mineral style that elevates it above the ordinary at an unusually fair price; 13% alcohol. I got mine for £4.50 on a win-double £6 offer amid a 25%-off-six promo.

AUSTRIA

🍷 **8** Taste the Difference Niederösterreich
Riesling 2020 £8.75

Lemon sherbet! A delightful Austrian spin on the Riesling theme tastes more like Austria's native Grüner Veltliner than traditional Riesling and there's no harm in that. It's so effervescent in mouthfeel, when you lift the glass to the light you expect to see it fizzing, but it's lake-still, and similarly refreshing and delightful; 12.5% alcohol.

WHITE WINES

🍷 10 Vouvray La Couronne des Plantagenets 2019 £7.25

Designated *Demi-sec* on the front label and 'medium sweet' on the back, I'd say this delightful Loire classic fits neither description. It is fresh, fruity and balanced – yes I know, these are universal terms – and in a wholesome style that defies further pigeon-holing. True, there is a honeyed aroma to the lush ripe-apple fruit, but there's charming citrus twang besides and a joyful easy weight with just 11.5% alcohol. Clearly it has a following, or Sainsbury's would have dumped it long ago, so I encourage adventurous drinkers wondering what might lie beyond Chardonnay, Pinot Grigio and Sauvignon to give this beautiful bargain Chenin Blanc a punt.

🍷 8 Taste the Difference Languedoc Blanc 2020 £7.50

This generously coloured and perfumed dry wine by Midi master Jean-Claude Mas is ripe with lush white stone and orchard fruits, weighty and indulgent; 13% alcohol. A constant bargain and not infrequently discounted.

🍷 9 Taste the Difference Côtes du Rhône Blanc 2020 £8.00

Utterly consistent since its introduction with the 2015 vintage, this lush dry wine makes a fine introduction to the underappreciated whites of the Côtes du Rhône, an appellation understandably dominated by production of distinctive, good-value reds. This wine is made for Sainsbury's by one of the region's leading growers, Gabriel Meffre, and it has distinctions of its own: fine gold colour, floral-nectar aromas and a plump, peachy ripeness enriched with oak contact and balanced with nectarine and citrus acidity; it tastes reassuringly expensive, combining gravitas with lively freshness; 12.5% alcohol.

WHITE WINES

8 **Baron de Guers Picpoul de Pinet 2020** £8.00
Full near-resiny ripe spin on the understandably popular
Picpoul theme; lemon-tangy and not punishingly dry – a
sort of Mediterranean Muscadet without the eyewatering
greenness; 13% alcohol. I paid £5.25 on promo.

8 **Taste the Difference Viognier 2020** £8.00
If you're expecting a sweet soft style from this, look
elsewhere. It's emphatically dry but with background
honey notes, apricot and pineapple and a distinct
nectarine-lime acidity that commands the overall picture.
Good aperitif wine with or without snackeroos; 13%
alcohol.

9 **Taste the Difference Petit Chablis 2019** £10.50
Recognisable gunflinty aroma on this immediately
impressive new vintage from the humblest of Chablis'
class-conscious collection of *appellations-contrôlées*. It's
lemon gold in colour and lemony-limey in the tang of its
sharp-apple fruit with a lick of exotic ripeness that is the
hallmark of these driest and crispest of classic Burgundy
Chardonnay wines – really very good indeed and sensibly
priced; 12% alcohol.

10 **Riesling Qualitätswein Rheinhessen 2019** £5.25
Soft but fresh, grapey rather than sweet, this crafty
contrivance from the Rhine vineyards is deliciously appley
and lush, just 9% alcohol, and a delectable aperitif.
The price seems ridiculously low for what is a genuine
quality wine from the world's noblest grape variety. Trad
Riesling lovers must try this.

WHITE WINES

Sainsbury's

GERMANY

🍷 9 **Sturmwolken Riesling 2020** £7.50
Modern-style fermented-out (11.5% alcohol) Rheinpfalz
newcomer, bristling with apple-crisp aromas and flavours,
full of freshness and zest. Fine dry but blossomy aperitif
wine at a keen price.

ITALY

🍷 8 **Rocca Murer Trentino Pinot Grigio 2020** £7.00
It's a reasonable rule that northerliness denotes degrees
of desirability in Italian Pinot Grigio. This one from sub-
Alpine Trentino by Anselmo Martini accordingly has
tangy-limey freshness alongside the floral-herby aromas
and fruit-basket melange of flavours; 12.5% alcohol.

🍷 7 **Taste the Difference Gavi 2020** £7.75
Brassica and grapefruit outline the flavour and acidity of
this Piedmontese dry wine by Araldica, lending it mild
distinction and interest; it's austere at first but reveals a
measure of white fruit to make it a partner for creamy
pastas and risotto; 12.5% alcohol.

NEW ZEALAND

🍷 8 **Yealands Sauvignon Blanc 2020** £8.00
Marlborough wine from an admired independent producer
now branching out into mass-market jazzily packaged
brands like this one. And it's a class act: cracklingly zingy
gooseberry brightness and nuanced herby-grassy-limey
fruitiness in ideal balance; 12.5% alcohol.

WHITE WINES

NEW ZEALAND

**9 Ara Select Blocks Organic
Sauvignon Blanc 2020** £12.00

Grand wine from the Wairau Valley in Marlborough is blended not just from distinct vineyard sites (blocks) but from different fermentation batches including must fermented with wild yeasts (cultured yeasts are near-universal these days) and barrel fermented. Experimental maybe but the wine is lush and clearly a cut above standard issue: classic gooseberry-grassy rush of green fruits with exciting glitter; 12.5% alcohol.

SPAIN

**8 Faustino Rivero Ulecia Albariño
Rias Baixas 2020** £12.00

Beautifully presented in a translucent ultramarine flûte bottle labelled in a very Spanish maritime style (great fish illustration) this pricy brand from the Atlantic-facing vineyards of Rias Baixas (pronounced 'ree-ass by-shass') in the breezy climes of Galicia just above Portugal's northern frontier is a work of art in its own right. The wine's pretty good too: salty seaside scents succeeded by breezy-fresh tangy white-fruit flavours with gentle citrus acidity; cries out for fishy dishes; 12.5% alcohol. A note on the choice of ultramarine blue for the bottle: 'ultramarine' doesn't mean preternaturally sea-blue, as might be supposed; it comes from the meaning 'beyond the sea' to describe the miraculous mineral lapis lazuli, source of the pigment hugely valued by artists in the earliest civilisations and latterly in the Italian Renaissance, mined in places unimaginably far distant beyond the sea – such as, er, Afghanistan. Wine and stories are such a good mix though, aren't they?

FORTIFIED WINES

9 **Taste the Difference Pale & Dry**
Fino Sherry 50cl £8.00
Cheerful new bottling for this Emilio Lustau sherry in a nicely sized 50cl bottle. It is every bit as pale and dry as advertised with plenty of pungent crispness and twang; 15% alcohol. It's brave of Sainsbury's to return to real sherry; they have launched and relaunched these 'premium' wines countless times over the decades to far too little acclaim.

SPARKLING WINES

10 **Sainsbury's Blanc de Noir**
Champagne Brut £21.00
Sommelier Holly Willcocks kindly reviewed *Best Wines 2021* on Instagram, quoting my description of this fine champagne's 'eager moose' and eliciting the response from one of her followers: 'What does an eager moose smell like?' Holly sportingly replied 'slightly sweaty from all the galloping'. And I thought I was the only wine writer who did jokes. Thank you, Holly, very much. I did, honestly, spell it mousse, but I wouldn't have missed this plaudit for anything. As to the champagne, it continues to be the best supermarket own-label of them all.

9 **Sainsbury's Demi-Sec Champagne** £19.00
The description *demi-sec* in some contexts denotes marked sweetness but this proper champagne made by respectable Louis Kremer is only a degree or two sweeter than *brut* styles (created in the late 1800s for the British market; hitherto all champagne had been sweet) and a deliciously mellow treat. You get full colour and mousse, an inviting digestive-bikkie nose, and mellow malic fruit – lovely; 12% alcohol. If you find some champagnes too 'green', give this bargain-priced rarity a try.

Tesco

 Subscribing as I do to Groucho Marx's famous axiom 'I refuse to join any club that would have me as a member', I have long resisted getting a supermarket loyalty card.

Until now. It started with the Co-op – clearly a worthy cause – and next came Waitrose (and Partners) out of solidarity, and the lure of a free newspaper. But the big one, in 2021, has been the Tesco Clubcard.

Frankly I don't know why I left it so long. Groucho's rebuff was to some ghastly cliquey club in America. Tesco Clubcard members in the UK alone (yes, there are overseas outcrops) number more than 17 million. I'm in.

There's a particular reason. Tesco has taken to restricting some of its more alluring wine offers to Clubcard holders. Actually they may have been doing it for years and I simply hadn't noticed. But now, given that I haven't been invited as an honoured member of the media to taste Tesco's wines for the last two years, why would I pass up the chance to get my necessary paid-for samples at a quid or two off? It is, in the current parlance, a no-brainer. Isn't that right, Lydia?

And so to this year's little selection, all obtained on discount either through my Clubcard or under the umbrella of one of the 25%-off-six offers Tesco has staged during 2021, usually in perfect synchrony with similar promotions at Sainsbury's, Morrisons, Asda and the rest.

Tesco wine seems to me to have survived the pandemic largely unscathed. Unlike at Sainsbury's, there seem to have been few serious losses to the excellent 'Finest' own-label range, and in the stores I have found most of the wines I set out for. Few new wines feature here this year, and I suspect that Tesco has probably put new lines on hold while the lingering effects of Covid-19 work their way out of the organism. If they ever do.

In the meantime, Tesco wine remains a safe bet. Don't hesitate to join in.

RED WINES

⟨8⟩ **Tesco Chilean Cabernet Sauvignon 2020** £3.89
The price looks like a leg-pull, but this is the genuine
article from Chile's sun-baked Central Valley, middling
in weight but wholesome in ripeness and grip with
familiar Cabernet blackcurrant and a lift of gentle spice
perhaps from the syrah grapes included in the blend;
12.5% alcohol.

⟨9⟩ **Tesco Beaujolais 2020** £5.00
Purple, juicy and bouncy with new-squished fruit, it's
distinctively delicious and sharpening, the best of red
wines to drink straight from the fridge; 12.5% alcohol.

⟨9⟩ **Reserve des Tuguets Madiran 2018** £7.00
New and much improved label design this year for a
Tesco stalwart of enduring allure. Made by Gascony's
Producteurs Plaimont from the Madiran AC's own
Tannat grape, it comes in an agreeably intense beetroot
shade with spicy sun-baked hedgerow-fruit aromas and
flavours and a friendly grip at the finish; 13% alcohol.

⟨8⟩ **Finest Côtes du Rhône Villages
Signargues 2019** £8.00
The 2019 harvest in the Rhône Valley has been the
fifth or sixth vintage of the century in succession, with
its distinguishing quality perhaps being the generous
ripeness of the reds from the southern reaches, known
as the Côtes. This one's a ready-rounded, bumper spicy
mouthfiller of very satisfying heft; 14.5% alcohol.

RED WINES

FRANCE

🍷 **10** **M Chapoutier Côtes du Rhône Villages 2019** £9.00

'If the 2019 has superseded [the 2018]' I counselled in last year's edition, 'take a chance'. Well it has and so have I, and it's without doubt my Rhône wine of the year. Plush wild blue/beeetroot colour and high-toned pruny nose; sweet-spice raspiness of black fruit in the mouth gives it an extraordinarily distinctive quality – an ideal partnering of intensity and edginess, the best possible match for richly flavoured dishes like the beef bourgignon we made mid-lockdown. A wine we won't forget in a hurry. It's generous in heft (15% alcohol) but beautifully poised. I paid £6.40 on offer, and that's mad.

🍷 **8** **Finest Montagne Saint-Emilion 2019** £9.00

A possibly-worthy successor to the marvellous 2018 was a tad raw with puckering tannin on tasting earlier in 2021 but had distinct prospects. Classy item with genuine St Emilion poise, good density of colour and mouthfeel, sleek blackberry fruit and well-managed oak definitely in need of time in the bottle; 13.5% alcohol. Buy now – the 2018 sold out very fast – and drink from 2022 at the earliest.

ITALY

🍷 **8** **Finest Montepulciano d'Abruzzo 2018** £7.00

Dependable brambly bouncy juice bomb of uplifting vivacity and redcurrant/raspberry savour; as fresh as a daisy and a good lightweight red to serve straight from the fridge on summery occasions; 12.5% alcohol. Nifty match for oily fish and salads as well as creamy pastas and sticky risotto. For my 2018 (still on shelf in summer 2021) I paid £4.50 on promo

RED WINES

ITALY

🍷 9 **Sette Muri Brindisi 2017**   £9.00
Brindisi is the historic seaport in Puglia at the end of ancient Rome's Appian Way. The local vineyards make fascinating red wines from Negroamaro grapes. Try this one, named Sette Muri after the seven walls that divide the vineyards, for size: it's dark, plush and earthily spicy with a marked pomegranate note amid the ripe blackberry aromas and flavours; trim tannin and 14% alcohol. I paid under £6 on promo.

🍷 9 **Finest Valpolicella Ripasso 2018**   £11.00
You can actually detect the bright-cherry juiciness of traditional Valpolicella in this trendy contrivance, made with the addition of concentrated grape must, so you get creamy richness and weight as well as the friendly features of the fondly remembered original. Really good spin by leading Verona co-op the Cantina Valpantena, with licorice-cinnamon notes and a nice firm grip at the edge of the flavour; 13.5% alcohol. Grilled meats, whiffy cheeses, tomato sauces on pasta.

PORTUGAL

🍷 9 **Tesco Douro 2019**   £6.00
Heady but by no means overweight table wine from the Port country has defined black-fruit flavours and the plummy-minty-spicy savours of the celebrated fortified wine without the fire of the spirit; at plonk price, you're getting a wine that tastes authentically of its place; 13% alcohol. Pleased to see Tesco's food-pairing suggestions include spicy sausages.

RED WINES

8 **Tesco Finest Douro 2019** £10.00

I do like the dreamy Douro Valley hillscape illustration on the label of this new wine which I hope won't displace my old friend Tesco Douro (above). This is a nice enough addition, though at a price two-thirds higher, not comparable for value. Colour, aroma and body speak of the intensity and minty spice of Port and it is satisfyingly complete; 13% alcohol. It's made by giant Sogrape, owner of Mateus Rosé and also of Sandeman – a Port producer of some reputation.

9 **Campaneo Old Vines Garnacha 2018** £5.00

Offered by Tesco maybe to defy Aldi/Lidl pricing, this bargain from Campo del Borja (a region renowned for Garnacha) does much better than that. The lurid red label intimates (to me) a wine that might be heatedly overripe, but it's a friendly juice-bomb with raspberry plumpness, spice and mint; 14% alcohol.

9 **Finest Viña del Cura Rioja Reserva 2016** £8.50

The plushest and silkiest yet among the long series of fine vintages for this house Rioja by serious bodega Baron de Ley. The fruit is darkly intense in its rich cassis savour, elevated by the new-oak-like vanilla shock in its delivery; 14% alcohol.

9 **Finest Viña del Cura Rioja Gran Reserva 2014** £11.50

Maturing succulent Baron de Ley wine is showing a little orange at the rim of the colour and taking on exotic aromatic-herb notes amid the cassis-and-cream intensity of fruit; 14% alcohol.

WHITE WINES

CHILE

🍷 **8**   **Tesco Chilean Chardonnay 2020**   **£3.99**
A cunningly contrived generic dry wine from Chile's vast
Central Valley vineyard zone; made without oak contact
but has a saucy note of exotic-fruit ripeness; 12.5%
alcohol. Top party white.

🍷 **10**   **Finest St Mont 2019**   **£6.50**
Perennial phenomenon from Producteurs Plaimont is a
wine for all seasons: autumn-gold colour, spring-blossom
floral aromas, summer-ripe fruit flavours encompassing
peach and pear, mango and melon, a lush reminder of
sunnier climes to see you through the bleak of winter;
13.5% alcohol. No kidding! I paid under a fiver for mine
on promo – a timeless bargain.

FRANCE

🍷 **9**   **Finest Côtes de Gascogne Blanc 2020**   **£6.50**
From Gascony's number one co-operative the Producteurs
Plaimont, a thrillingly lively limey dry wine with lush
underlying apple-crisp fruit all at a very keen price;
11.5% alcohol. I got mine in a blanket promo at under
a fiver.

🍷 **8**   **Finest Picpoul de Pinet 2020**   **£7.50**
This generous green-gold Mediterranean oyster-matcher
is on good form again, as piquant in its briny freshness
as the name alludes, with a well-judged citrus uplift; 13%
alcohol.

WHITE WINES

FRANCE

🍷 **10 Guigal Côtes du Rhône Blanc 2018** £12.00
This is lush! Expensive lemon-gold colour, promising canteloupe melon and peach aromas, big mouthful of creamily-rich but tangily lifted white fruits in ideal balance, it's long, sumptuous and lingering in its savour; 14% alcohol. Guigal is one of the Rhône Valley's grander producers and also makes more white wine than any of the competition. I'd say they're out on their own with this one, made as it is with 60% Viognier, 25% Roussanne and Marsanne and (among the rest of the blend) just 2% Grenache Blanc, the grape that constitutes the greater part of most other Côtes du Rhône Blanc. I call this wine a proper discovery.

ITALY

🍷 **8 Finest Pecorino 2020** £7.00
Abruzzo dry wine has a sort of spearmint savour that veers just short of sweet, lifted by a grapefruit-like acidity. Sounds complicated but it's a fun food white in its own way, nice match for chicken as well as saucy compilations or mild-mannered fishy dishes; 13% alcohol. I paid £4.50 on promo. That's cheap.

SPAIN

🍷 **9 Tesco Viña del Cura Rioja Blanco 2019** £5.00
I've been overlooking this junior member of Tesco's excellent own-label Rioja line-up. It's remarkably fresh, lush and tangy, a proper modern unoaked rendering of the interesting Viura grape, and remarkably cheap too; 12.5% alcohol. Not branded in the Tesco Finest range, but easily the best-value new-style white Rioja in the supermarkets.

WHITE WINES

SPAIN

🍷 **8**   **Finest Viñas del Rey Albariño 2020**   **£8.50**
Bold, bracing Atlantic-coast wine from Rias Baixas region is almost saline in its seaside zest, full of exuberant tangy flavours with underlying notes of nectarine and grapefruit, even a tweet of honeysuckle; 12.5% alcohol. Good assertive partner to oysters, mussels and whelks, natch. I paid just over £6 on promo – good deal.

FORTIFIED WINES

PORTUGAL

🍷 **10**   **Finest 10-Year-Old Tawny Port**   **£12.00**
I lie awake at night worrying whether this is the same wine as Morrisons' 10-Year-Old Tawny. Like the Morrisons' version, it's made by Symingtons and the same price at £12. But I believe it is a shade richer and just that much more spicily rounded and warm; 20% alcohol. Definitely a moot port.

SPAIN

🍷 **10**   **Finest Fino Sherry 37.5cl**   **£6.00**
Bone-dry, scintillatingly fresh, tangy and agreeably pungent pale sherry by Gonzalez Byass has more than a passing similarity to that great bodega's flagship fino Tio Pepe, and that's just fine as far as I'm concerned. At £6 for a half-bottle it costs about the same, too. But never mind that – this is world-class wine at any price.

SPARKLING WINES

9 **Finest 1531 Blanquette de Limoux Brut** £9.50
The price is up 50p on last year, but this is still a top buy in the fizz firmament. Limoux in the foothills of the Pyrenees is locally claimed as the cradle of sparkling wine, production beginning in 1531 at a Benedictine priory – 150 years earlier than a similar effervescence was revealed by monks in Champagne. This is an excellent example with abounding mousse, eager crisp white fruit, jangling freshness; 12.5% alcohol.

10 **Finest Premier Cru Champagne Brut** £20.00
I marvel at the consistency of this seriously good champagne, always full and generous in its bready aromas, creaming sparkle and lush ripe fruits mellowed with long bottle ageing. The grapes for it really do come from superior premier cru vineyards – the term does have meaning in Champagne – and even from top-rate grand cru vineyards as well; 12.5% alcohol. The standard price is a gift and I got my bottle this year on promo for a ridiculous £13.50.

9 **Finest Vintage Grand Cru Blanc de Blancs Champagne Brut 2013** £26.00
The 2012 vintage seemed to go on for ever – I first reviewed it in *Best Wines 2019* – and the new 2013 will surely do likewise, certainly in terms of development in bottle if not time on the shelf. It's a fine, sweet-brioche-nosed, broad-flavoured already-rounded lemon-topped champagne of obvious quality and charm; 12.5% alcohol.

SPARKLING WINES

FRANCE

🍷 9 **Lanson Le Black Label Champagne Brut**   £33.00
I bought this at Easter when it was reduced to £25 on individual promo then to £18.75 in the 25% off any six bottles blanket deal. It was a good buy as this famous NV wine, formerly known as Lanson Black Label (spot the difference?), is on terrific form right now, delivering an attention-grabbing balance of freshness and lusciously ripe white and exotic fruits in a deluxe rush of microbubbles; 12.5% alcohol.

───────*Waitrose*───────

Waitrose (& Partners) has continued to weather the debilitating effects of Covid, sporadic lockdowns and the separation from Ocado with uninterrupted aplomb. In the wine department, that is. There have, of course, been plunging profits (and partners' profit shares), and store closures in the wider John Lewis context, but the grocery side of the business seems enduringly serene.

There is no danger of Waitrose losing its prime position, in this guide at least, among supermarket wine retailers. There are still more than a thousand different lines to choose from and even the more modestly sized stores among the total of about 340 branches carry a pretty decent choice. This is really not the case with any of Waitrose's rivals.

The myth that Waitrose is pricier than those rivals continues, however, to prevail. All I can say with conviction is that this does not apply to the wines. In fairness, Waitrose eschews most of the dismal global brands that crowd other supermarkets' shelves, but where there is coincidence, I can find no significant price differential.

And Waitrose does not disdain price promotion on wines. There is a rolling monthly selection of scores of bottles on individual promotion, and every now and then in week-long gaps between these promos, a blanket offer of 25% off everything if you buy six or more bottles. It might be cribbed from Sainsbury's and Tesco, but who's complaining?

Now in case you're thinking all this sounds a bit of a glowing encomium for Waitrose, let me tell you about my own experience of one of these blanket offers. I decided to take advantage by ordering my wine bargains online for home delivery (free if you spend more than £150). I duly filled in the form online and sent it on the first day of the promo week. Got an email confirmation. Then got a phone call. We're sorry. A couple of the wines for which they had accepted my order weren't in fact available. What would I like them to do? Well send me what you've got, I said. I was worried the offer would have lapsed by the time they delivered. Had visions of being charged the full price.

Well, delivery didn't take place till long after the offer had lapsed. But they took the money for the whole order at the original price, including the wines not delivered. I was a bit tired of it all by now so I didn't even bother taking it up with them. In future though, I think I'll stick to shopping in person. Many of the wines described in the following pages were from that order, and I really mustn't complain.

RED WINES

AUSTRALIA

🍷 8 **Botham The All-Rounder Cabernet Sauvignon 2020** £7.99

Picked this up for £5.99 on offer and it wasn't bad: middling in colour-density and weight rather than beefy but wholesome in its blackberry ripeness with artful caramel and mint, it's easy to like even if it mightn't bowl you over; 13% alcohol.

🍷 8 **Summer Road Old Vine Grenache 2020** £8.49

Unusually for anything sub-£10 from Oz (I paid £7.49 on promo) an interesting and characterful wine from a non-mainstream grape variety. In keeping with the Grenache's indigenous Rhône manifestations it's light to look at, soft but defined in its perky redcurrant juiciness and not without woof at 14.5% alcohol. I do agree with the Waitrose buyer that it chills well.

🍷 10 **Wirra Wirra Church Block 2018** £13.49

Fabled McLaren Vale blend of Cabernet Sauvignon, Shiraz and Merlot, dependably generous in its spicy lusciousness, long blackcurrant and blackberry flavours and perfectly contrived tannins for a textbook tight finish; 14.5% alcohol. Waitrose have followed this famous brand for ever and are perpetually discounting it. I paid £9.99 for mine. Surely one of the great Aussie bargains.

CHILE

🍷 8 **LFE Bin 77 Malbec 2020** £8.99

I paid just £5.99 on promo for this Central Valley wine from sizeable but still-family-owned producer Luis Felipe Edwards and at that price it's pretty good: wholesome baked plum pie style, easy spice and nicely integrated and long in flavour, trim with gentle tannin, really quite beguiling; 13% alcohol. At full price it's just as impressive of course, but less impressive for value.

RED WINES

Waitrose

CHILE

🍷 7   LFE Bin 31 Merlot 2020   £8.99
Also picked up for £5.99 on promo, a lightweight cherry-fruit picnic red for outdoor occasions, could be served chilled. A bit lean for my taste, but an honest attempt at easy-drinking Merlot making more price sense at £6 than £9; 13.5% alcohol.

FRANCE

🍷 6   Cuvée des Vignerons Beaujolais   £7.79
This ordinary light cherry-raspberry Beaujolais of the kind that benefits from moderate chilling has long been non-vintage but in 2021 seems a bit leaner than of memory. Last time round I said this wine was produced for Waitrose by Georges Duboeuf but the current bottling is by Jean Gamet; 12.5% alcohol. The price isn't warranted: other supermarket own-labels at around a fiver are just as good as this.

🍷 6   Fitou Mme Claude Parmentier 2018   £8.49
Revival of a once-cult Mediterranean brand that back in the 1970s led the way for Midi wines into export markets but got left behind in the end, this is a simple red-fruit spicy number of nostalgic charm but really rather lacking in modern merit; 12.5% alcohol. It doesn't warrant the price.

🍷 9   Rémy Ferbras Ventoux 2019   £8.99
Another spiffing new vintage for this distinctive Rhône/Provence frontier AC which I note is 14.5% alcohol, well up on the 2018's 13% but by no means overdone. In fact it's juicy, slinky and spicily delectable in the reassuring Mediterranean tradition, a fine match, as the maker avers on the back label, for shepherd's pie. Look out for regular promo pricing to £6.99.

RED WINES

10 Saumur Les Nivières 2018   **£9.99**

An outstanding 100% Cabernet Franc from the Loire Valley and on top form in this vintage: deep purple colour, enticing new-squished berry aromas and eager, luscious highly distinctive refreshingly bright purple-tasting fruit with hallmark leafy abrasion to the grippy finish; 12.5% alcohol. Top match for summer cold cuts, saucy fish dishes, pongy cheeses and a great wine to drink cool on warmer days. I believe this vintage will repay keeping two or more years to mellow a bit.

**9   Cairanne Réserve des Hospitaliers Cru
      des Côtes du Rhône 2019**   **£11.99**

Epic vintage for this hugely enjoyable senior Rhône wine. It has pitch-dark crimson colour, big licorice and damson honk and gripping spicy savours in the best tradition, hefted with oak contact and 14.5% alcohol. The Hospitaliers in the name were reportedly crusading knights from Cairanne (now a top village wine *cru* of the Rhône) tasked with defending a Christian hospital in Jerusalem in the 12th century. Why am I telling you this? Anyway, it has noble character and will age well into the 21st century.

**9   Mas des Montagnes Terroirs d'Altitude
      Côtes du Roussillon Villages 2016**   **£11.99**

Handsomely packaged Pyrennean wine with instant appeal: deep purple colour, mountain-herb and wild blackfruit perfume, vivid but yielding corresponding berry fruit flavours and a dignified damson-plum intensity; charming Mediterranean wine for charcuterie, interesting cheeses and fish pie; 14.5% alcohol.

FRANCE

RED WINES

FRANCE

🍷 8 **St Joseph Cave de St Desirat 2019**   £15.99
St Joseph, says Waitrose, is arguably the best-value appellation of the northern Rhône Valley. Given the prices demanded for the red wines of neighbouring Cornas and Côte Rôtie, Hermitage and even Crozes-Hermitage, I can see what they mean. This wine, pure Syrah as all the red wines of these great ACs are, is a pretty nifty introduction to the regional style. Again I agree with Waitrose's own claim of 'warm raspberry and blackberry-fruit flavours streaked with hints of liquorice'. It's elegantly weighted, slinky and an obvious match for roast meats or a nice fillet steak; 14.5% alcohol.

🍷 7 **Gigondas Le Roc des Dentelles 2017**   £22.49
It is axiomatic that Gigondas is among the highest-priced of the senior southern Rhône village appellations because is it easier to pronounce than the names of most of its rivals. But 22 quid is a lot to ask for a wine only a short step up from the rabble. I went mad and paid £15.49 for this on promo, and can report that it's a nicely focused wine from a jolly good harvest year with the benefit of some bottle age, easily worth half the full price being asked. It's made by ubiquitous Gabriel Meffre, producer of countless Rhône brands, and in a nice embossed bottle; 14.5% alcohol.

GREECE

🍷 8 **Tsantali Organic Cabernet Sauvignon 2019**   £9.99
Fine new vintage for this perennial favourite from the northern seaside region of Halkidiki. It has slinky blackcurrant ripeness to its long, elegant flavours, finishing brightly clean; 13% alcohol.

RED WINES

ITALY

8 Maree d'ione Nero di Troia 2019   £8.79

Easy-going Puglian red from organically grown Nero di Troia grapes offering dark plummy gently spicy brisk-finishing flavours with a lick of creamy smoothness from oak contact; 13% alcohol.

9 Recchia Bardolino 2020   £8.79

This lovely cherry-bright classic refresher from Verona delicately balances sweet redcurrant-cherry ripeness with crisp acidity. Pale in jewel-like ruby colour, it has gentle creamy nuttiness of aroma and lipsmacking berry-fruit savour. There's nothing quite like it; 12.5% alcohol. Serve cool. I paid just £6.49 on promo.

10 Salice Salentino Borgodei Trulli 2019   £8.99

If anything, an even better vintage for this Puglian prodigy than last year's triumph, so 10 points. It's darkly dense, brightly aromatic and wildly savoury of blackberry, blueberry and prune and perfectly weighted; faithful to the best Italian tradition of focused slinky juiciness, keen-edge acidity and friendly closing tannins, a fine match for indigenous cuisine; 13.5% alcohol. It is perpetually discounted on promo to £6.99 but top-scores at full price anyway. When the offer's on, buy in bulk. In my local Waitrose it sells out at alarming speed.

RED WINES

9 Triade Rosso 2018   £8.99

From Puglia, a blend of – you'll have guessed – three grape varieties (Negroamaro, Primitivo and Nero di Troia) forming a richly crimson-hued, spikily perfumed blackberry-cherry-spicy whole of deliciously savoury and slinky character, finishing with classic Italian tannin-grip dryness; 13.5% alcohol. Adaptable pasta, barbecue and rich-stew match. I paid £6.74 on promo.

8 Stemmari Nero d'Avola   £8.99

Nice big whack of sun-baked blackberry fruit right at the front of this friendly Sicilian's vivid flavour – you're drawn in at once to the spicy depths. Very nicely weighted wine that, if anything, improved on reopening next day (handy screwcap), rounding and mellowing into long briary flavours; 13% alcohol. I paid £6.74 on promo.

**10 Terre di Faiano Primitivo
       Organic Wine 2020**   £9.99

It's made by the appassimento method, a technique pioneered in Verona, now catching on in Puglia, home of this sumptuous wine, which Waitrose bills as the 'first organic Primitivo made 100% by the appassimento method'. Now there's a boast for you. It is soupy dense and plump, rich with suggestions of dark chocolate, autumnally spicy and rich but finishing with briskly gripping soft tannins and particularly poised in this new 2020 vintage; 13.5% alcohol. Regularly discounted to £7.99.

7 Firriato Le Sabbie dell'Etna 2018   £10.99

Handsomely presented volcano red with an unexpectedly pale hue and lightness of being, accompanied by a burnt-earth spiciness and brambly fruit; 13.5% alcohol. It's probably perfectly good of its kind but I was disappointed, consoled only by the fact that I'd got it on promo for £7.75.

RED WINES

**9 Bersano Piandelpiete Dolcetto
d'Asti 2018**   **£11.99**

Really attractive example of Piedmont's Dolcetto grape
with vivid purple colour and an eager, cranberry whiff en
route to the juicy-bouncy morello cherry fruit elegantly
trimmed with a sweet-tannin edge; lovely match for an
interesting risotto (most risottos are not interesting) and
doubly virtuous for its capacity to stimulate and refresh;
12.5% alcohol. Stands out.

10 Cantina del Nebb Nebbiolo 2018   **£12.99**

Gosh this is classy, says my effusive note. Typical
translucent jewel-ruby colour, aroma of intense red-
cherry and rose petal, the Nebbiolo signature, and a
beautifully defined succulent fruit with notions of mocha,
pomegranate and redcurrant; there's no other way of
putting it: it's elegant. It's heady, too, and tastes very
expensive even though it's a fraction of the price of the
grand Piedmont Nebbiolo reds Barolo and Barbaresco –
many of which in my experience fall short of the appeal
of this delightful pure varietal by Alba's own co-operative
the Cantine del Nebbiolo; 14.5% alcohol. The perfect red
wine for roast birds, game or fowl. I paid £9.74 for mine
on promo. Bargain of the year?

10 Masi Campofiorin Rosso del Verona 2017 £12.99

This enduring oddity (first produced in 1964) from grand
Verona outfit Masi is a sort of supercharged Valpolicella,
grounded in the cherry brightness of the base wine,
fermented with the addition of concentrated must into a
dark, cushiony style redolent of sweet plum, cinnamon,
violets and marzipan, fringed with gentle tannin grip and
nutskin dryness at the finish; 13% alcohol. A different
spin on the current amarone/ripasso craze and frequently
reduced on promo to an alluring £9.74.

ITALY

RED WINES

NEW ZEALAND

🍷 8 **The Ned Pinot Noir 2019** £13.49

I've been meaning to try this for years, if only on account of the outstandingly alluring name. It's middling in weight and intensity (but 13.5% alcohol) and eagerly vivid with cherry-raspberry juiciness in the approved Kiwi manner. Even though it's quite a pricy item, I'd be inclined to drink it straight from the fridge as a cool match for white meats, oily fish or chicken dishes.

SOUTH AFRICA

🍷 8 **John X Merriman Rustenberg 2019** £15.99

Remarkably rounded and developed Bordeaux-like wine from a grand Stellenbosch estate established in 1892 by one John Xavier Merriman, who served as the last premier of the 'Cape Colony' before the founding of South Africa. This Cabernet-led blend really does replicate the claret style; I am just mystified how, in such youth, it can resemble a mature Bordeaux. Convincing, full of cassis charm and 14% alcohol.

SPAIN

🍷 8 **Heredad del Rey Reservada Yecla 2019** £6.99

The Yecla DO neighbours better-known Jumilla near Alicante and deserves more attention, especially for wines from Monastrell grapes (same variety as Mourvèdre of southern France). This one is rather magnificent both in its bold retro packaging and gripping savours of black cherry, warm spice and even black pepper, smoothed with a bit of oak ageing into a distinctive whole; 13.5% alcohol. Authentic paella partner.

RED WINES

SPAIN

8 Familia Pacheco Monastrell 2019   **£7.99**
Sinewy Jumilla in a brightly packaged screwcap bottle
complete with a red tractor on the label; organically
made and boldly fruity with roasted-berry savours and
plenty of woof (14% alcohol). A natural match for
spicy dishes and incinerated barbecue offerings.

8 Castillo de Olite Navarra Tinto 2015   **£8.99**
An old favourite that's been radically restyled label-wise
but still delivers the familiar sweetly ripe cassis flavours
smoothed with lengthy oak contact. Although 2015 was
a hyped vintage in Navarra (neighbour to Rioja) this is
noticeably less intense than the 2013 (overall a poorly
rated year) I much liked last year, but it's poised and
likeable, with 13.5% alcohol. Shelf price is down from
£9.49 last year (it was £9.99 in 2019) and I paid just
£6.99 on promo.

7 Beronia Rioja Crianza 2017   **£11.99**
I paid £7.99 on promo for this ambitiously priced crianza
from a bodega owned by sherry bodega Gonzalez Byass.
It's sleek and lively with blackcurrant juiciness but
somehow plausible rather than convincing; for the price
I was expecting something exceptional; 13.5% alcohol.

9 Torres Celeste Crianza 2017   **£12.99**
Astral Ribera del Duero by Catalan star Miguel Torres;
has a fully orbital label depicting the night sky and a
correspondingly decorated cork that sprinkled annoying
dust into the wine when extracted. But never mind that,
it's a fine oaked pure Tempranillo of slinky pruny-
mulberry intensity and tastes heavenly; 14% alcohol.
The price is by no means astronomical for this quality,
especially if, like me, you wait for the regular promo deal
at just under £10.

Waitrose

RED WINES

SPAIN

🍷 9 La Petite Agnès Priorat 2017   **£14.99**

Priorat is the former wilderness region of Catalonia lost to the world of wine when phylloxera laid waste to the vineyards more than a century ago. Enterprising growers began to revive viticulture on the revered *licorella* soils from the 1980s and now the region can rival Rioja or the Ribera del Duero for quality – and price. Most small-estate Priorat is lethally expensive, but here's a dark, spicily savoury, silkily oaked and intensely black-fruit minerally pure example at a sensible price; 15% alcohol.

PINK WINES

ENGLAND

🍷 8 Simpsons Rosé 2020   **£14.99**

I had not previously known that Waitrose lists a hundred different English wines until I picked this one out to taste on Channel Four's *Sunday Brunch* programme. I thought I ought to mention Waitrose's stalwart support of our native vignerons, who include enterprising couple Charles and Ruth Simpson, makers of this fine rosé on the North Downs of Kent. Made from their Pinot Noir vines (mainly dedicated to sparkling-wine production), it has a delicate salmon-pink colour, alluring floral-strawberry perfume and refreshing floral red-fruit style, crisp and dry; 12.5% alcohol. It's expensive, of course, but at least was on promo at £11.99 when the programme went out.

WHITE WINES

ARGENTINA

🍷 8   **Santa Julia Torrontes 2020**   **£9.49**

Argentina's signature white grape Torrontes, often compared to the Muscat of France, here makes an exotic and honey-scented dry wine with an artful balance of lushness and refreshment; organically made by the pioneering (and enduring) La Agricola winery of Mendoza and generously ripe at 14% alcohol. I paid a bargain £6.99 on promo.

AUSTRALIA

🍷 9   **Cumulus Vineyards Climbing Chardonnay 2018**   **£9.99**

Oaked Chardonnay led Australia's original ascent to first place in the UK market. History now, of course, but here's a nostalgic recollection from New South Wales, creamy with new-oak slink but busting out all over with exotic sweet-apple-melon-quince fresh flavours and clean citrus edge; 12.5% alcohol. Curious-looking package, but an elevating wine indeed.

CHILE

🍷 8   **Errazuriz Costa Sauvignon Blanc 2020**   **£11.99**

From coastal vineyards facing the South Pacific ocean, an untypical Chilean Sauvignon pinging with sea-breeze piquancy more than tropical ripeness and excitingly fresh with grassy, nettle zest and long lemony aftertastes; 13% alcohol. Really quite special, which I suppose it needs to be at the price.

WHITE WINES

10 Cuvée Pêcheur 2020 £5.49

The first among the customer reviews of this perennial stalwart on Waitrose's website describes it in glowing terms, beginning 'This Sauvignon Blanc …'. Fair comment, I say, even though it's made entirely from Ugni Blanc and Colombard grapes grown in Gascon vineyards once known for producing little other than utilitarian plonk for distilling into Armagnac brandy. Now, the region excels at everyday bargain white table wines such as this meadow-scented, grassy-fresh and delightfully tangy Sauvignon-free blend at a giveaway price; 11.5% alcohol.

8 Picpoul de Pinet Les Canots 2020 £8.49

Big-flavoured, saline, almost resiny take on the madly popular Picpoul theme has a positive sour-apple twang and eager green freshness without being too challenging. 'French retsina' Mrs Halley called it, not without a note of affection. It will certainly stand up to any of the fishy flavours for which it is supposed to be the ideal partner, even the ghastly muddy lagoon oysters of the AC's nearby Mediterranean resort Sète, but best of all with proper dry-smoked trout and the like; 12.5% alcohol.

9 Waitrose Blueprint White
Burgundy 2019 £9.49

Generic Chardonnay identified as Mâcon-Lugny, well-coloured and alluringly scented with sweet apple ripeness leading to elegant matching flavours extending to peaches and a little creaminess, all this conveyed on a fine frame of minerality; 13% alcohol. Tastes well above price.

WHITE WINES

8 **Cave de Beblenheim Kleinfels Riesling 2019** £10.99

Alsace Riesling vigorously asserts the regional style with racy crisp-apple aromas and fruit, spicy intensity and lifting citrus (grapefruit here) acidity; 13% alcohol. Dry but aromatic and a versatile food matcher: anything from smoked fish to roast chicken or duck.

9 **Paul Blanck Gewürztraminer 2019** £14.99

Waitrose's mainly excellent range of Alsace wines includes the ubiquitous Türckheim co-operative Gewürz (£10.99), which you should avoid in favour of this proper estate wine from Domaine Blanck, est 1610 and run today by Philippe Blanck, Qigong master and inspired winetreprenur. This is textbook Gewurz, 'very rich and decadent' in Waitrose's words, but also brightly balanced, lush rather than sweet, spicy, smoky and wild with lychee and rose-petal aromatics; 13% alcohol.

9 **Pinot Gris Urmeer 2020** £7.99

In Germany the Pinot Gris grape of France is usually known as Ruländer or Grauerburgunder. Wise of this wine's producer Reh Kendermann, then, to adopt the crisper French moniker for this one. The style of the wine is not dissimilar to that of its Alsace manifestation. It's rich in colour and tone, plump with sweet orchard fruit and contrastingly mineral with citrus twangs; 12.5% alcohol. See if you can find the 'oatmeal notes' spoken of by Waitrose.

FRANCE

GERMANY

WHITE WINES

ITALY

🍷 8 Alta Italia Pinot Grigio 2020 £9.99

The first Pinot Grigio I have bought in years, this cost me £6.66 on promo. It's from the Trentino which, as the name Alta Italia implies, is in the high country of Italy's sub-Alpine north. It owes something in its smokiness of style to the Pinot Gris (same grape) of Alsace, a bit further north and west, though with less emphasis on acidity. Nice full, aromatic aperitif with notions of sweet pear, grapefruit and melon and more interesting than your average Veneto PG; 12.5% alcohol.

NEW ZEALAND

🍷 8 The Ned Pinnacle Sauvignon Blanc 2020 £12.99

Top-of-the-range wine from hugely popular and brilliantly named (after a mountain peak) Marlborough wine upstages less-elevated standard The Ned Sauvignon Blanc with big gooseberry-limey perfume, emphatic corresponding mouthfilling, green-grass lush savours and a luxurious plumpness contributed by oak contact – and lengthy refreshment; 13.5% alcohol.

SPAIN

🍷 9 Beronia Rueda Verdejo 2019 £8.99

Beronia's the producer, Rueda the region (just south of Ribera del Duero) and Verdejo's the grape. The wine is Spain's answer to world-conquering Sauvignon Blanc, and this one's a very decent effort: bold colour, potent perfume of peachy-melon ripeness picked up in the generous but vividly zesty grassy lushness of the flavour, lifted by citrus twang; 13% alcohol. Yup, I liked it. Beronia is a brand name of top sherry bodega Gonzalez Byass so this is a diversion, and a welcome one.

FORTIFIED WINES

**10 Waitrose Amontillado Medium
Dry Sherry** £7.69

Sherry militants might warn you this is 'sweetened' and not, as proper amontillado ought to be, entirely dry to the taste. Heed them nought. This Blueprint own-label is made by blending a bit of rich PX (Pedro Ximenez grape) wine alongside the oxidising bone-dry Palomino Fino wine that customarily comprises the entirety of approved amontillado. It has a glowing conker colour, heady sweet-nut and fruit-compote aroma and gloriously pungent-but-rich smoky-roasty flavours; sublime balance and 18.5% alcohol. This is sherry for purists and amateurs alike, made by Waitrose's long-time partner Sanchez-Romate in Jerez. Drink in decent-size wine glasses straight from the fridge on any occasion you can think of.

**10 Cayetano del Pino Y Cia Very Old
Palo Cortado Solera 37.5cl** £10.99

Grown-up sherry of awe-inspiring bronze-gold colour, pungent aroma and glorious preserved fruit and toasted-nut savours. Has a bright note of fresh-strawberry sweetness, a fine introduction to the rarest of natural sherry styles, palo cortado. It's dry but unfathomably complex and nuanced; 20% alcohol. Serve well-chilled as you would a fino. Our bottle (thank you, Max) had a haze to the colour but it did not detract. The next one (thank you again, Max) was fully bright.

SPAIN

SPARKLING WINES

FRANCE

Waitrose

🍷 10 Cave de Lugny Crémant de Bourgogne Blanc de Blancs £13.99

This perpetually discounted creamily sparkling Mâconnais Chardonnay is a consistent delight. Lush with sweet-apple ripeness and busy in its persistent mousse, it has perky citrus lift, perfectly dry but generous in its flow of flavour; 12% alcohol. It's not imitation champagne, it has its own charms, and at the regular promo price of £10.49 it's one of the best fizz buys from anywhere.

🍷 7 Waitrose Blanc de Noir Champagne Brut £23.99

Pure Pinot Noir champagne can thrill, but my 2021 tasting of this hardy perennial brought me up short. Where it has been 'movingly mellow and calming' (2019 report) it seemed tired and faintly oxidative, and the mousse was less than vivacious from the start; 12% alcohol.

Enjoying it

Drink or keep?

Wines from supermarkets should be ready to drink as soon as you get them home. Expensive reds of recent vintage, for example from Bordeaux or the Rhône, sold as seasonal specials, might benefit from a few years' 'cellaring'. If in doubt, look up your purchase on a web vintage chart to check.

Some wines certainly need drinking sooner than others. Dry whites and rosés won't improve with time. Good-quality red wines will happily endure, even improve, for years if they're kept at a constant moderate temperature, preferably away from bright light, and on their sides so corks don't dry out. Supermarkets like to advise us on back labels of red wines to consume the product within a year or two. Pay no attention.

Champagne, including supermarket own-label brands, almost invariably improves with keeping. Evolving at rest is what champagne is all about. Continue the process at home. I like to wait for price promotions, buy in bulk and hoard the booty in smug certainty of a bargain that's also an improving asset. None of this applies to any other kind of sparkling wine – especially prosecco.

Of more immediate urgency is the matter of keeping wine in good condition once you've opened it. Recorked leftovers should last a day, but after that the wine will oxidise, turning stale and sour. There is a variety of wine-saving stopper devices, but I have yet to find one that works. My preferred method is to decant leftovers into a smaller bottle with a pull-cork or screwcap. Top it right up.

Early opening

Is there any point in uncorking a wine in advance to allow it to 'breathe'? Absolutely none. The stale air trapped between the top of the wine and the bottom of the cork (or screwcap) disperses at once and the 1cm circle of liquid exposed will have a negligible response to the atmosphere. Decanting the wine will certainly make a difference, but whether it's a beneficial difference is a matter for conjecture – unless you're decanting to get the wine off its lees or sediment.

Beware trying to warm up an icy bottle of red. If you put it close to a heat source, take the cork out first. As the wine warms, even mildly, it gives off gas that will spoil the flavour if it cannot escape.

Chill factor

White wine, rosé and sparkling wines all need to be cold. It's the law. The degree of chill is a personal choice but icy temperatures can mask the flavours of good wines. Bad wines, on the other hand, might benefit from overchilling. The anaesthetic effect removes the sense of taste.

Red wines can respond well to mild chilling. Beaujolais and stalky reds of the Loire such as Chinon and Saumur are brighter when cool, as is Bardolino from Verona and lighter Pinot Noir from everywhere.

Is it off?

Once there was a plague of 'corked' wine. It's over. Wine bottlers have eliminated most of the causes. Principal among them was TCA or trichloroanisole 123, an infection of the raw material from which corks are made, namely the bark of cork oak trees. New technology developed by firms such as Portuguese cork giant Amorim has finally made all cork taint-free.

TCA spawned an alternative-closure industry that has prospered mightily through the supply of polymer stoppers and screwcaps. The polymer products, although unnecessary now that corks are so reliable, persist. They're pointless: awkward to extract and to reinsert, and allegedly less environmentally friendly than natural corks.

Screwcaps persist too, but they have their merits. They obviate the corkscrew and can be replaced on the bottle. They are recyclable. Keep them on the bottles you take to the bottle bank.

Some closures will, of course, occasionally fail due to material faults or malfunctions in bottling that allow air into the bottle. The dull, sour effects on wine of oxidation are obvious, and you should return any offending bottle to the supplier for a replacement or refund. Supermarkets in my experience are pretty good about this.

Wines that are bad because they are poorly made are a bit more complicated. You might just hate it because it's not to your taste – too sweet or too dry, too dense or too light – in which case, bad luck. But if it has classic (though now rare) faults such as mustiness, a vinegar taint (volatile acidity or acetate), cloudiness or a suspension of particles, don't drink it. Recork it and take it back to the supplier.

Glass action

There is something like a consensus in the wine world about the right kind of drinking glass. It should consist of a clear, tulip-shaped bowl on a comfortably long stem. You hold the glass by the stem so you can admire the colour of the wine and keep the bowl free of fingermarks. The bowl is big enough to hold a sensible quantity of wine at about half full. Good wine glasses have a fine bevelled surface at the rim of the bowl. Cheap glasses have a rolled rim that catches your lip and, I believe, materially diminishes the enjoyment of the wine.

Good wine glasses deserve care. Don't put them in the dishwasher. Over time, they'll craze. To maintain the crystal clarity of glasses wash them in hot soapy water, rinse clean with hot water and dry immediately with a glass cloth kept exclusively for this purpose. Sounds a bit nerdy maybe, but it can make all the difference.

What to eat with it?

When tasting a hundred or more wines one after the other and trying to make lucid notes on each of them, the mind can crave diversion. Besides describing the appearance, aroma and taste, as I'm supposed to do, I often muse on what sort of food the wine might suit.

Some of these whimsical observations make it into the finished reports for this book. Like all the rest of it, they are my own subjective opinion, but maybe they help set the wines in some sort of context.

Conventions such as white wine with fish and red with meat might be antiquated, but they can still inhibit choice. If you only like white wine must you abstain on carnivorous occasions – or go veggie? Obviously not. Much better to give detailed thought to the possibilities, and go in for plenty of experimentation.

Ripe whites from grapes such as Chardonnay can match all white meats, cured meats and barbecued meats, and most saucy meat dishes too. With bloody chunks of red meat, exotic whites from the Rhône Valley or Alsace or oaky Rioja Blanco all come immediately to mind.

As for those who prefer red wine at all times, there are few fish dishes that spurn everything red. Maybe a crab salad or a grilled Dover sole. But as soon as you add sauce, red's back on the menu. Again, the answer is to experiment.

Some foods do present particular difficulties. Nibbles such as salty peanuts or vinegary olives will clash with most table wines. So buy some proper dry sherry, chill it down and thrill to the world's best aperitif. Fino, manzanilla and amontillado sherries of real quality now feature in all the best supermarkets – some under own labels.

Eggs are supposed to be inimical to wine. Boiled, fried or poached certainly. But an omelette with a glass of wine, of any colour, is surely a match. Salads, especially those with fruit or tomatoes, get the thumbs-down, but I think it's the dressing. Forgo the vinegar, and salad opens up a vinous vista.

Cheese is a conundrum. Red wine goes with cheese, right? But soft cheeses, particularly goat's, can make red wines taste awfully tinny. You're much better off with an exotic and ripe white wine. Sweet white wines make a famously savoury match with blue cheeses. A better match, I believe, than with their conventional companions, puddings. Hard cheeses such as Cheddar may be fine with some red wines, but even better with a glass of Port.

Wine with curry? Now that incendiary dishes are entirely integrated into the national diet, I suppose this is, uh, a burning question. Big, ripe reds such as Australian Shiraz can stand up to Indian heat, and Argentine Malbec seems appropriate for chilli dishes. Chinese cuisine likes aromatic white wines such as Alsace (or New Zealand) Gewürztraminer, and salsa dishes call for zingy dry whites such as Sauvignon Blanc.

But everyone to their own taste. If there's one universal convention in food and wine matching it must surely be to suit yourself.

—A Wine Vocabulary—

A brief guide to the use of language across the wine world – on labels, in literature and among the listings in this book

A

AC – *See* Appellation d'Origine Contrôlée.

acidity – Natural acids in grape juice are harnessed by the winemaker to produce clean, crisp flavours. Excess acidity creates rawness or greenness; shortage is indicated by wateriness.

aftertaste – The flavour that lingers in the mouth after swallowing or spitting the wine.

Aglianico – Black grape variety of southern Italy. Vines originally planted by ancient Greek settlers from 600BC in the arid volcanic landscapes of Basilicata and Cilento produce distinctive dark and earthy reds.

Agriculture biologique – On French wine labels, an indication that the wine has been made by organic methods.

Albariño – White grape variety of Spain that makes intriguingly perfumed fresh and tangy dry wines, especially in esteemed Atlantic-facing Rias Baixas region.

alcohol – The alcohol levels in wines are expressed in terms of alcohol by volume ('abv'), that is, the percentage of the volume of the wine that is common, or ethyl, alcohol. A typical wine at 12 per cent abv is thus 12 parts alcohol and, in effect, 88 parts fruit juice. Alcohol is viewed by some health professionals as a poison, but there is actuarial evidence that total abstainers live shorter lives than moderate consumers. The UK Department of Health declares there is no safe level of alcohol consumption, and advises that drinkers should not exceed a weekly number of 'units' of alcohol. A unit is 10ml of pure alcohol, the quantity contained in about half a 175ml glass of wine with 12 per cent alcohol. From 1995, the advisory limit on weekly units was 28 for men and 21 for women. This was reduced in 2016 to 14 for men and women alike.

Alentejo – Wine region of southern Portugal (immediately north of the Algarve), with a fast-improving reputation, especially for sappy, keen reds from local grape varieties including Aragones, Castelão and Trincadeira.

Almansa – DO winemaking region of Spain inland from Alicante, making inexpensive red wines.

Alsace – France's easternmost wine-producing region lies between the Vosges Mountains and the River Rhine, with Germany beyond. These conditions make for the production of some of the world's most delicious and fascinating white wines, always sold under the name of their constituent grapes. Pinot Blanc is the most affordable – and is well worth looking out for. The 'noble' grape varieties of the region are Gewürztraminer, Muscat, Riesling and Pinot Gris and they are always made on a single-variety basis. The richest, most exotic wines are those from individual *grand cru* vineyards, which are named on the label. Some *vendange tardive* (late harvest) wines are made, and tend to be expensive. All the wines are sold in tall, slim green bottles known as flûtes that closely resemble those of the Mosel. The names of producers as well as grape varieties are often German too, so it is widely assumed that Alsace wines are German in style, if not in nationality. But this is not the case in either particular. Alsace wines are dry and quite unique in character – and definitely French.

amarone – Style of red wine made in Valpolicella, Italy. Specially selected grapes are held back from the harvest and stored for several months to dry them out. They are then pressed and fermented into a highly concentrated speciality dry wine. Amarone means 'bitter', describing the dry style of the flavour.

amontillado – *See* sherry.

aperitif – If a wine is thus described, I believe it will give as much pleasure before a meal as with one. Crisp, low-alcohol German wines and other delicately flavoured whites (including many dry Italians) are examples.

appassimento – Italian technique of drying out new-picked grapes to concentrate the sugars. Varying proportions of appassimento fruit are added to the fermentation of speciality wines such as amarone and ripasso.

Appellation d'Origine Contrôlée – Commonly abbreviated to AC or AOC, this is the system under which top-quality wines have been defined in France since 1935. About a third of the country's vast annual output qualifies across about 500 AC (or AOP – see Appellation d'Origine Protégée) zones. The declaration of an AC on the label signifies that the wine meets standards concerning location of vineyards and wineries, grape varieties and limits on harvest per hectare, methods of cultivation and vinification, and alcohol content. Wines are inspected and tasted by state-appointed committees.

Appellation d'Origine Protégée (AOP) – Under European Union rule changes, the AOC system is gradually transforming into AOP. In effect, it means little more than the exchange of 'controlled' with 'protected' on labels. One quirk of the rules is that makers of AOP wines will be able to name the constituent grape variety or varieties on their labels, if they so wish.

Apulia – Anglicised name for Puglia, Italy.

Aragones – Synonym in Portugal, especially in the Alentejo region, for the Tempranillo grape variety of Spain.

Ardèche – Region of southern France to the west of the Rhône river, home to a good IGP zone including the Coteaux de l'Ardèche. Decent-value reds from Syrah and Cabernet Sauvignon grapes, and less interesting dry whites.

Arneis – White grape variety of Piedmont, north-west Italy. Makes dry whites with a certain almondy richness at often-inflated prices.

Assyrtiko – White grape variety of Greece now commonly named on dry white wines, sometimes of great quality, from the mainland and islands.

Asti – Town and major winemaking centre in Piedmont, Italy. The sparkling (spumante) wines made from Moscato grapes are inexpensive and sweet with a modest 5 to 7 per cent alcohol. Vivid red wine Barbera d'Asti also produced.

attack – In wine-tasting, the first impression made by the wine in the mouth.

Auslese – German wine-quality designation. *See* QmP.

B

Baga – Black grape variety indigenous to Portugal. Makes famously concentrated, juicy reds of deep colour from the grapes' particularly thick skins. Look out for this name, now quite frequently quoted as the varietal on Portuguese wine labels.

balance – A big word in the vocabulary of wine tasting. Respectable wine must get two key things right: lots of fruitiness from the sweet grape juice, and plenty of acidity so the sweetness is 'balanced' with the crispness familiar in good dry whites and the dryness that marks out good reds. Some wines are noticeably 'well balanced' in that they have memorable fruitiness and the clean, satisfying 'finish' (last flavour in the mouth) that ideal acidity imparts.

Barbera – Black grape variety originally of Piedmont in Italy. Most commonly seen as Barbera d'Asti, the vigorously fruity red wine made around Asti – once better known for sweet sparkling Asti Spumante. Barbera grapes are now cultivated in South America, producing less-interesting wine than at home in Italy.

Bardolino – Once fashionable, light red wine DOC of Veneto, north-west Italy. Bardolino is made principally from Corvina Veronese grapes plus Rondinella, Molinara and Negrara. Best wines are supposed to be those labelled Bardolino Superiore, a DOCG created in 2002. This classification closely specifies the permissible grape varieties and sets the alcohol level at a minimum of 12 per cent.

Barossa Valley – Famed vineyard region north of Adelaide, Australia, produces hearty reds principally from Shiraz, Cabernet Sauvignon and Grenache grapes, plus plenty of lush white wine from Chardonnay. Also known for limey, long-lived, mineral dry whites from Riesling grapes.

barrique – Barrel in French. *En barrique* on a wine label signifies the wine has been matured in casks rather than tanks.

Beaujolais – Unique red wines from the southern reaches of Burgundy, France, are made from Gamay grapes. Beaujolais nouveau, now unfashionable, provides a friendly introduction to the bouncy, red-fruit style of the wine, but for the authentic experience, go for Beaujolais Villages, from the region's better, northern vineyards. There are ten AC zones within this northern sector making wines under their own names. Known as the *crus*, these are Brouilly, Chénas, Chiroubles, Côte de Brouilly, Fleurie, Juliénas, Morgon, Moulin à Vent, Regnié and St Amour. Prices are higher than those for Beaujolais Villages, but not always justifiably so.

Beaumes de Venise – Village near Châteauneuf du Pape in France's Rhône valley, famous for sweet and alcoholic wine from Muscat grapes. Delicious, grapey wines. A small number of growers also make strong (sometimes rather tough) red wines under the village name.

Beaune – One of the two centres (the other is Nuits St Georges) of the Côte d'Or, the winemaking heart of Burgundy in France. Three of the region's humbler appellations take the name of the town: Côtes de Beaune, Côtes de Beaune Villages and Hautes Côtes de Beaune.

berry fruit – Some red wines deliver a burst of flavour in the mouth that corresponds to biting into a newly picked berry – strawberry, blackberry, etc. So a wine described as having berry fruit (by this writer, anyway) has freshness, liveliness and immediate appeal.

bianco – White wine, Italy.

Bical – White grape variety principally of Dão region of northern Portugal. Not usually identified on labels, because most of it goes into inexpensive sparkling wines. Can make still wines of very refreshing crispness.

biodynamics – A cultivation method taking the organic approach several steps further. Biodynamic winemakers plant and tend their vineyards according to a date and time calendar 'in harmony' with the movements of the planets. Some of France's best-known wine estates subscribe, and many more are going that way. It might all sound bonkers, but it's salutary to learn that biodynamics is based on principles first described by the eminent Austrian educationist Rudolf Steiner.

bite – In wine-tasting, the impression on the palate of a wine with plenty of acidity and, often, tannin.

blanc – White wine, France.

blanc de blancs – White wine from white grapes, France. May seem to be stating the obvious, but some white wines (e.g. champagne) are made, partially or entirely, from black grapes.

blanc de noirs – White wine from black grapes, France. Usually sparkling (especially champagne) made from black Pinot Meunier and Pinot Noir grapes, with no Chardonnay or other white varieties.

blanco – White wine, Spain and Portugal.

Blauer Zweigelt – Black grape variety of Austria, making a large proportion of the country's red wines, some of excellent quality.

Bobal – Black grape variety mostly of south-eastern Spain. Thick skin is good for colour and juice contributes acidity to blends.

bodega – In Spain, a wine producer or wine shop.

Bonarda – Black grape variety of northern Italy. Now more widely planted in Argentina, where it makes some well-regarded red wines.

botrytis – Full name, *botrytis cinerea*, is that of a beneficent fungus that can attack ripe grape bunches late in the season, shrivelling the berries to a gruesome-looking mess, which yields concentrated juice of prized sweetness. Cheerfully known as 'noble rot', this fungus is actively encouraged by winemakers in regions as diverse as Sauternes (in Bordeaux), Monbazillac (in Bergerac), the Rhine and Mosel valleys, Hungary's Tokaji region and South Australia to make ambrosial dessert wines.

bouncy – The feel in the mouth of a red wine with young, juicy fruitiness. Good Beaujolais is bouncy, as are many north-west-Italian wines from Barbera and Dolcetto grapes.

Bourgogne Grand Ordinaire – Former AC of Burgundy, France. *See* Coteaux Bourguignons.

Bourgueil – Appellation of Loire Valley, France. Long-lived red wines from Cabernet Franc grapes.

briary – In wine tasting, associated with the flavours of fruit from prickly bushes such as blackberries.

brûlé – Pleasant burnt-toffee taste or smell, as in crème brûlée.

brut – Driest style of sparkling wine. Originally French, for very dry champagnes specially developed for the British market, but now used for sparkling wines from all round the world.

Buzet – Little-seen AC of south-west France overshadowed by Bordeaux but producing some characterful ripe reds.

C

Cabardès – AC for red and rosé wines from area north of Carcassonne, Aude, France. Principally Cabernet Sauvignon and Merlot grapes.

Cabernet Franc – Black grape variety originally of France. It makes the light-bodied and keenly edged red wines of the Loire Valley – such as Chinon and Saumur. And it is much grown in Bordeaux, especially in the appellation of St Emilion. Also now planted in Argentina, Australia and North America. Wines, especially in the Loire, are characterised by a leafy, sappy style and bold fruitiness. Most are best enjoyed young.

Cabernet Sauvignon – Black (or, rather, blue) grape variety now grown in virtually every wine-producing nation. When perfectly ripened, the grapes are smaller than many other varieties and have particularly thick skins. This means that when pressed, Cabernet grapes have a high proportion of skin to juice – and that makes for wine with lots of colour and tannin. In Bordeaux, the grape's traditional home, the grandest Cabernet-based wines have always been known as *vins de garde* (wines to keep) because they take years, even decades, to evolve as the effect of all that skin extraction preserves the fruit all the way to magnificent maturity. But in today's impatient world, these grapes are exploited in modern winemaking techniques to produce the sublime flavours of mature Cabernet without having to hang around for lengthy periods awaiting maturation. While there's nothing like a fine, ten-year-old claret (and few quite as expensive), there are many excellent Cabernets from around the world that amply illustrate this grape's characteristics. Classic smells and flavours include blackcurrants, cedar wood, chocolate, tobacco – even violets.

Cahors – An AC of the Lot Valley in south-west France once famous for 'black wine'. This was a curious concoction of straightforward wine mixed with a soupy must, made by boiling up new-pressed juice to concentrate it (through evaporation) before fermentation. The myth is still perpetuated that Cahors wine continues to be made in this way, but production on this basis actually ceased 150 years ago. Cahors today is no stronger, or blacker, than the wines of neighbouring appellations. Principal grape variety is Malbec, known locally as Cot.

Cairanne – Village of the appellation collectively known as the Côtes du Rhône in southern France. Cairanne is one of several villages entitled to put their name on the labels of wines made within their AC boundary, and the appearance of this name is quite reliably an indicator of quality.

Calatayud – DO (quality wine zone) near Zaragoza in the Aragon region of northern Spain where they're making some astonishingly good wines at bargain prices, mainly reds from Garnacha and Tempranillo grapes. These are the varieties that go into the polished and oaky wines of Rioja, but in Calatayud, the wines are dark, dense and decidedly different.

Cannonau – Black grape native to Sardinia by name, but in fact the same variety as the ubiquitous Grenache of France (and Garnacha of Spain).

cantina sociale – *See* co-op.

Carignan – Black grape variety of Mediterranean France. It is rarely identified on labels, but is a major constituent of wines from the southern Rhône and Languedoc-Roussillon regions. Known as Carignano in Italy and Cariñena in Spain.

Cariñena – A region of north-east Spain, south of Navarra, known for substantial reds, as well as the Spanish name for the Carignan grape (*qv*).

Carmenère – Black grape variety once widely grown in Bordeaux but abandoned due to cultivation problems. Lately revived in South America where it is producing fine wines, sometimes with echoes of Bordeaux.

cassis – As a tasting note, signifies a wine that has a noticeable blackcurrant-concentrate flavour or smell. Much associated with the Cabernet Sauvignon grape.

Castelao – Portuguese black grape variety. Same as Periquita.

Catarratto – White grape variety of Sicily. In skilled hands it can make anything from keen, green-fruit dry whites to lush, oaked super-ripe styles. Also used for Marsala.

cat's pee – In tasting notes, a jocular reference to the smell of a certain style of Sauvignon Blanc wine.

cava – The sparkling wine of Spain. Most originates in Catalonia, but the Denominación de Origen (DO) guarantee of authenticity is open to producers in many regions of the country. Much cava is very reasonably priced even though it is made by the same method as champagne – second fermentation in bottle, known in Spain as the *método clásico*.

CdR – Côtes du Rhône. My own shorthand.

cépage – Grape variety, French. 'Cépage Merlot' on a label simply means the wine is made largely or exclusively from Merlot grapes.

Chablis – Northernmost AC of France's Burgundy region. Its dry white wines from Chardonnay grapes are known for their fresh and steely style, but the best wines also age very gracefully into complex classics.

Chambourcin – Sounds like a cream cheese but it's a relatively modern (1963) French hybrid black grape that makes some good non-appellation lightweight-but-concentrated reds in the Loire Valley and now some heftier versions in Australia.

champagne – The sparkling wine of the strictly defined Champagne region of France, made by the equally strictly defined champagne method.

Chardonnay – Possibly the world's most popular grape variety. Said to originate from the village of Chardonnay in the Mâconnais region of southern Burgundy, the vine is now planted in every wine-producing nation. Wines are commonly characterised by generous colour and sweet-apple smell, but styles range from lean and sharp to opulently rich. Australia started the craze for oaked Chardonnay, the gold-coloured, super-ripe, buttery 'upfront' wines that are a caricature of lavish and outrageously expensive burgundies such as Meursault and Puligny-Montrachet. Rich to the point of egginess, these Aussie pretenders are now giving way to a sleeker, more minerally style with much less oak presence – if any at all. California and Chile, New Zealand and South Africa are competing hard to imitate the Burgundian style, and Australia's success in doing so.

Châteauneuf du Pape – Famed appellation centred on a picturesque village of the southern Rhône valley in France where in the 1320s French Pope Clement V had a splendid new château built for himself as a summer retreat amidst his vineyards. The red wines of the AC, which can be made from 13 different grape varieties but principally Grenache, Syrah and Mourvèdre, are regarded as the best of the southern Rhône and have become rather expensive – but they can be sensationally good. Expensive white wines are also made.

Chenin Blanc – White grape variety of the Loire Valley, France. Now also grown farther afield, especially in South Africa. Makes dry, soft white wines and also rich, sweet styles.

cherry – In wine tasting, either a pale red colour or, more commonly, a smell or flavour akin to the sun-warmed, bursting sweet ripeness of cherries. Many Italian wines, from lightweights such as Bardolino and

Valpolicella to serious Chianti, have this character. 'Black cherry' as a description is often used of Merlot wines – meaning they are sweet but have a firmness of mouthfeel associated with the thicker skins of black cherries.

Cinsault – Black grape variety of southern France, where it is invariably blended with others in wines of all qualities from country reds to pricy appellations such as Châteauneuf du Pape. Also much planted in South Africa. The effect in wine is to add keen aromas (sometimes compared with turpentine) and softness to the blend. The name is often spelt Cinsaut.

Clape, La – A small *cru* (defined quality-vineyard area) within the Coteaux du Languedoc where the growers make some seriously delicious red wines, mainly from Carignan, Grenache and Syrah grapes. A name worth looking out for on labels from the region.

claret – The red wine of Bordeaux, France. Old British nickname from Latin *clarus*, meaning 'clear', recalling a time when the red wines of the region were much lighter in colour than they are now.

clarete – On Spanish labels indicates a pale-coloured red wine. Tinto signifies a deeper hue.

classed growth – English translation of French *cru classé* describes a group of 60 individual wine estates in the Médoc district of Bordeaux, which in 1855 were granted this new status on the basis that their wines were the most expensive of the day. The classification was a promotional wheeze to attract attention to the Bordeaux stand at that year's Great Exhibition in Paris. Amazingly, all of the wines concerned are still in production and most still occupy more or less their original places in the pecking order price-wise. The league was divided up into five divisions from *Premier Grand Cru Classé* (just four wines originally, with one promoted in 1971 – the only change ever made to the classification) to *Cinquième Grand Cru Classé*. Other regions of Bordeaux, notably Graves and St Emilion, have since imitated Médoc and introduced their own rankings of *cru classé* estates.

classic – An overused term in every respect – wine descriptions being no exception. In this book, the word is used to describe a very good wine of its type. So, a 'classic' Cabernet Sauvignon is one that is recognisably and admirably characteristic of that grape.

Classico – Under Italy's wine laws, this word appended to the name of a DOC or DOCG zone has an important significance. The classico wines of the region can only be made from vineyards lying in the best-rated areas, and wines thus labelled (e.g. Chianti Classico, Soave Classico, Valpolicella Classico) can be reliably counted on to be a cut above the rest.

Colombard – White grape variety of southern France. Once employed almost entirely for making the wine that is distilled for armagnac and cognac brandies, but lately restored to varietal prominence in the Côtes de Gascogne where high-tech wineries turn it into a fresh and crisp, if unchallenging, dry wine at a budget price. But beware, cheap Colombard (especially from South Africa) can still be very dull.

Conca de Barbera – Winemaking region of Catalonia, Spain.

co-op – Very many of France's good-quality, inexpensive wines are made by co-operatives. These are wine-producing centres whose members, and joint-owners, are local *vignerons* (vine growers). Each year they sell their harvests to the co-op for turning into branded wines. In Italy, co-op wines can be identified by the words *Cantina Sociale* on the label and in Germany by the term *Winzergenossenschaft*.

Corbières – A name to look out for. It's an AC of France's Midi (deep south) and produces countless robust reds and a few interesting whites, often at bargain prices.

Cortese – White grape variety of Piedmont, Italy. At its best, makes delicious, keenly brisk and fascinating wines, including those of the Gavi DOCG. Worth seeking out.

Costières de Nîmes – Until 1989, this AC of southern France was known as the Costières de Gard. It forms a buffer between the southern Rhône and Languedoc-Roussillon regions, and makes wines from broadly the same range of grape varieties. It's a name to look out for, the best red wines being notable for their concentration of colour and fruit, with the earthy-spiciness of the better Rhône wines and a likeable liquorice note. A few good white wines, too, and even a decent rosé or two.

Côte – In French, it simply means a side, or slope, of a hill. The implication in wine terms is that the grapes come from a vineyard ideally situated for maximum sunlight, good drainage and the unique soil conditions prevailing on the hill in question. It's fair enough to claim that vines grown on slopes might get more sunlight than those grown on the flat, but there is no guarantee whatsoever that any wine labelled 'Côtes du' this or that is made from grapes grown on a hillside anyway. Côtes du Rhône wines are a case in point. Many 'Côtes' wines come from entirely level vineyards and it is worth remembering that many of the vineyards of Bordeaux, producing most of the world's priciest wines, are little short of prairie-flat. The quality factor is determined much more significantly by the weather and the talents of the winemaker.

Coteaux Bourguignons – Generic AC of Burgundy, France, since 2011 for red and rosé wines from Pinot Noir and Gamay grapes, and white wines from (principally) Chardonnay and Bourgogne Aligoté grapes. The AC replaces the former appellation Bourgogne Grand Ordinaire.

Côtes de Blaye – Appellation Contrôlée zone of Bordeaux on the right bank of the River Gironde, opposite the more prestigious Médoc zone of the left bank. Best-rated vineyards qualify for the AC Premières Côtes de Blaye. A couple of centuries ago, Blaye (pronounced 'bligh') was the grander of the two, and even today makes some wines that compete well for quality, and at a fraction of the price of wines from its more fashionable rival across the water.

Côtes de Bourg – AC neighbouring Côtes de Blaye, making red wines of decent quality and value.

Côtes du Luberon – Appellation Contrôlée zone of Provence in south-east France. Wines, mostly red, are similar in style to Côtes du Rhône.

Côtes du Rhône – One of the biggest and best-known appellations of south-east France, covering an area roughly defined by the southern reaches of the valley of the River Rhône. The Côtes du Rhône AC achieves notably consistent quality at all points along the price scale. Lots of brilliant-value warm and spicy reds, principally from Grenache and Syrah grapes. There are also some white and rosé wines.

Côtes du Rhône Villages – Appellation within the larger Côtes du Rhône AC for wine of supposed superiority made in a number of zones associated with a long list of nominated individual villages.

Côtes du Roussillon – Huge appellation of south-west France known for strong, dark, peppery reds often offering very decent value.

Côtes du Roussillon Villages – Appellation for superior wines from a number of nominated locations within the larger Roussillon AC. Some of these village wines can be of exceptional quality and value.

crianza – Means 'nursery' in Spanish. On Rioja and Navarra wines, the designation signifies a wine that has been nursed through a maturing period of at least a year in oak casks and a further six months in bottle before being released for sale.

cru – A word that crops up with confusing regularity on French wine labels. It means 'the growing' or 'the making' of a wine and asserts that the wine concerned is from a specific vineyard. Under the Appellation Contrôlée rules, countless *crus* are classified in various hierarchical ranks. Hundreds of individual vineyards are described as *premier cru* or *grand cru* in the classic wine regions of Alsace, Bordeaux, Burgundy and Champagne. The common denominator is that the wine can be counted on to be expensive. On humbler wines, the use of the word *cru* tends to be mere decoration.

cru classé – *See* classed growth.

cuve – A vat for wine. French.

cuvée – French for the wine in a *cuve*, or vat. The word is much used on labels to imply that the wine is from just one vat, and thus of unique, unblended character. *Première cuvée* is supposedly the best wine from a given pressing because it comes from the free-run juice of grapes crushed by their own weight before pressing begins. Subsequent *cuvées* will have been from harsher pressings, grinding the grape pulp to extract the last drops of juice.

D

Dão – Major wine-producing region of northern Portugal now turning out much more interesting reds than it used to – worth looking out for anything made by mega-producer Sogrape.

demi sec – 'Half-dry' style of French (and some other) wines. Beware. It can mean anything from off-dry to cloyingly sweet.

DO – Denominación de Origen, Spain's wine-regulating scheme, similar to France's AC, but older – the first DO region was Rioja, from 1926. DO wines are Spain's best, accounting for a third of the nation's annual production.

DOC – Stands for Denominazione di Origine Controllata, Italy's equivalent of France's AC. The wines are made according to the stipulations of each of the system's 300-plus denominated zones of origin, along with a further 74 zones, which enjoy the superior classification of DOCG (DOC with *e Garantita* – guaranteed – appended).

DOCa – *Denominación de Origen Calificada* is Spain's highest regional wine classification; currently only Priorat and Rioja qualify.

DOP – Denominazione di Origine Protetta is an alternative classification to DOC (*qv*) under EU directive in Italy, comparable to AOP (*qv*) in France, but not yet widely adopted.

Durif – Rare black grape variety mostly of California, where it is also known as Petite Sirah, with some plantings in Australia.

E

earthy – A tricky word in the wine vocabulary. In this book, its use is meant to be complimentary. It indicates that the wine somehow suggests the soil the grapes were grown in, even (perhaps a shade too poetically) the landscape in which the vineyards lie. The amazing-value red wines of the torrid, volcanic southernmost regions of Italy are often described as earthy. This is an association with the pleasantly 'scorched' back-flavour in wines made from the ultra-ripe harvests of this near-sub-tropical part of the world.

edge – A wine with edge is one with evident (although not excessive) acidity.

élevé – 'Brought up' in French. Much used on wine labels where the wine has been matured (brought up) in oak barrels, *élevé en fûts de chêne*, to give it extra dimensions.

Entre Deux Mers – Meaning 'between two seas', it's a region lying between the Dordogne and Garonne rivers of Bordeaux, now mainly known for dry white wines from Sauvignon Blanc and Semillon grapes.

Estremadura – Wine-producing region occupying Portugal's coastal area north of Lisbon. Lots of interesting wines from indigenous grape varieties, often at bargain prices. If a label mentions Estremadura, it is a safe rule that there might be something good within.

Extremadura – Minor wine-producing region of western Spain abutting the frontier with Portugal's Alentejo region. Not to be confused with Estremadura of Portugal (above).

F

Falanghina – Revived ancient grape variety of southern Italy now making some superbly fresh and tangy white wines.

Faugères – AC of the Languedoc in south-west France. Source of many hearty, economic reds.

Feteasca – White grape variety widely grown in Romania. Name means 'maiden's grape' and the wine tends to be soft and slightly sweet.

Fiano – White grape variety of the Campania of southern Italy and Sicily, lately revived. It is said to have been cultivated by the ancient Romans for a wine called Apianum.

finish – The last flavour lingering in the mouth after wine has been swallowed.

fino – Pale and very dry style of sherry. You drink it thoroughly chilled – and you don't keep it any longer after opening than other dry white wines. Needs to be fresh to be at its best.

Fitou – AC of Languedoc, France. Red wines principally from Carignan, Grenache, Mourvèdre and Syrah grapes.

flabby – Fun word describing a wine that tastes dilute or watery, with insufficient acidity.

Frappato – Black grape variety of Sicily. Light red wines.

fruit – In tasting terms, the fruit is the greater part of the overall flavour of a wine. The wine is, after all, composed entirely of fruit

G

Gamay – The black grape that makes all red Beaujolais and some ordinary burgundy. It is a pretty safe rule to avoid Gamay wines from other regions.

Garganega – White grape variety of the Veneto region of north-east Italy. Best known as the principal ingredient of Soave, but occasionally included in varietal blends and mentioned as such on labels. Correctly pronounced 'gar-GAN-iga'.

Garnacha – Spanish black grape variety synonymous with Grenache of France. It is blended with Tempranillo to make the red wines of Rioja and Navarra, and is now quite widely cultivated elsewhere in Spain to make grippingly fruity varietals.

garrigue – Arid land of France's deep south giving its name to a style of red wine that notionally evokes the herby, heated, peppery flavours associated with such a landscape and its flora. A tricky metaphor.

Gavi – DOCG for dry aromatic white wine from Cortese grapes in Piedmont, north-west Italy. Trendy Gavi di Gavi wines tend to be enjoyably lush, but are rather expensive.

Gewürztraminer – One of the great grape varieties of Alsace, France. At their best, the wines are perfumed with lychees and are richly, spicily fruity, yet quite dry. Gewürztraminer from Alsace can be expensive, but the grape is also grown with some success in Germany, Italy, New Zealand and South America, at more approachable prices. Pronounced 'ge-VOORTS-traminner'.

Givry – AC for red and white wines in the Côte Chalonnaise sub-region of Burgundy. Source of some wonderfully natural-tasting reds that might be lighter than those of the more prestigious Côte d'Or to the north, but have great merits of their own. Relatively, the wines are often underpriced.

Glera – New official name for the Prosecco grape of northern Italy.

Godello – White grape variety of Galicia, Spain.

Graciano – Black grape variety of Spain that is one of the minor constituents of Rioja. Better known in its own right in Australia where it can make dense, spicy, long-lived red wines.

green – I don't often use this in the pejorative. Green, to me, is a likeable degree of freshness, especially in Sauvignon Blanc wines.

Grecanico – White grape variety of southern Italy, especially Sicily. Aromatic, grassy dry white wines.

Greco – White grape variety of southern Italy believed to be of ancient Greek origin. Big-flavoured dry white wines.

Grenache – The mainstay of the wines of the southern Rhône Valley in France. Grenache is usually the greater part of the mix in Côtes du Rhône reds and is widely planted right across the neighbouring Languedoc-Roussillon region. It's a big-cropping variety that thrives even in the hottest climates and is really a blending grape – most commonly with Syrah, the noble variety of the northern Rhône. Few French wines are labelled with its name, but the grape has caught on in Australia in a big way and it is now becoming a familiar varietal, known for strong, dark liquorous reds. Grenache is the French name for what is originally a Spanish variety, Garnacha.

Grillo – White grape of Sicily said to be among the island's oldest indigenous varieties, pre-dating the arrival of the Greeks in 600 BC. Much used for fortified Marsala, it has lately been revived for interesting, aromatic dry table wines.

grip – In wine-tasting terminology, the sensation in the mouth produced by a wine that has a healthy quantity of tannin in it. A wine with grip is a good wine. A wine with too much tannin, or which is still too young (the tannin hasn't 'softened' with age) is not described as having grip, but as mouth-puckering – or simply undrinkable.

Grolleau – Black grape variety of the Loire Valley principally cultivated for Rosé d'Anjou.

Gros Plant – White grape variety of the Pays Nantais in France's Loire estuary; synonymous with the Folle Blanche grape of south-west France.

Grüner Veltliner – The 'national' white-wine grape of Austria. In the past it made mostly soft, German-style everyday wines, but now is behind some excellent dry styles, too.

H

halbtrocken – 'Half-dry' in Germany's wine vocabulary. A reassurance that the wine is not a sugared Liebfraumilch-style confection.

hard – In red wine, a flavour denoting excess tannin, probably due to immaturity.

Haut-Médoc – Extensive AC of Bordeaux accounting for the greater part of the vineyard area to the north of the city of Bordeaux west of the Gironde river. The Haut-Médoc incorporates the prestigious commune-ACs of Listrac, Margaux, Moulis, Pauillac, St Estèphe and St Julien.

Hermitage – AC of northern Rhône Valley, France for red wines from Syrah grapes and some whites. Hermitage is also the regional name in South Africa for the Cinsaut grape.

hock – The wine of Germany's Rhine river valleys. Traditionally, but no longer consistently, it comes in brown bottles, as distinct from the wine of the Mosel river valleys – which comes in green ones.

Hunter Valley – Long-established (1820s) wine-producing region of New South Wales, Australia.

I

Indicación Geográfica Protegida (IGP) – Spain's country-wine quality designation covers 46 zones across the country. Wines made under the IGP can be labelled Vino de la Tierra.

Indication Géographique Protégée (IGP) – Introduced to France in 2010 under EU-wide wine-designation rules, IGP covers the wines previously known as vins de pays. Some wines are currently labelled IGP, but established vins de pays producers are redesignating slowly, if at all, and are not obliged to do so. Some will abbreviate, so, for example, Vin de Pays d'Oc shortens to Pays d'Oc.

Indicazione Geografica Tipica (IGT) – Italian wine-quality designation, broadly equivalent to France's IGP. The label has to state the geographical location of the vineyard and will often (but not always) state the principal grape varieties from which the wine is made.

isinglass – A gelatinous material used in fining (clarifying) wine. It is derived from fish bladders and consequently is eschewed by makers of 'vegetarian' or 'vegan' wines.

J

jammy – The 'sweetness' in dry red wines is supposed to evoke ripeness rather than sugariness. Sometimes, flavours include a sweetness reminiscent of jam. Usually a fault in the winemaking technique.

Jerez – Wine town of Andalucia, Spain, and home to sherry. The English word 'sherry' is a simple mispronunciation of Jerez.

joven – Young wine, Spanish. In regions such as Rioja, *vino joven* is a synonym for *sin crianza*, which means 'without ageing' in cask or bottle.

Jura – Wine region of eastern France incorporating four AOCs, Arbois, Château-Chalon, Côtes du Jura and L'Etoile. Known for still red, white and rosé wines and sparkling wines as well as exotic *vin de paille* and *vin jaune*.

Jurançon – Appellation for white wines from Courbu and Manseng grapes at Pau, south-west France.

K

Kabinett – Under Germany's bewildering wine-quality rules, this is a classification of a top-quality (QmP) wine. Expect a keen, dry, racy style. The name comes from the cabinet or cupboard in which winemakers traditionally kept their most treasured bottles.

Kekfrankos – Black grape variety of Hungary, particularly the Sopron region, which makes some of the country's more interesting red wines, characterised by colour and spiciness. Same variety as Austria's Blaufrankisch.

L

Ladoix – Unfashionable AC at northern edge of Côtes de Beaune makes some of Burgundy's true bargain reds. A name to look out for.

Lambrusco – The name is that of a black grape variety widely grown across northern Italy. True Lambrusco wine is red, dry and very slightly sparkling, and enjoying a current vogue in Britain.

Languedoc-Roussillon – Extensive wine region of southern France incorporating numerous ACs and IGP zones, notably the Pays d'Oc and Côtes de Roussillon.

lees – The detritus of the winemaking process that collects in the bottom of the vat or cask. Wines left for extended periods on the lees can acquire extra dimensions of flavour, in particular a 'leesy' creaminess.

legs – The liquid residue left clinging to the sides of the glass after wine has been swirled. The persistence of the legs is an indicator of the weight of alcohol. Also known as 'tears'.

lieu dit – This is starting to appear on French wine labels. It translates as an 'agreed place' and is an area of vineyard defined as of particular character or merit, but not classified under wine law. Usually, the *lieu dit*'s name is stated, with the implication that the wine in question has special merit.

liquorice – The pungent, slightly burnt flavours of this confection are detectable in some wines made from very ripe grapes, for example, the Malbec harvested in Argentina and several varieties grown in the very hot vineyards of southernmost Italy. A close synonym is 'tarry'. This characteristic is by no means a fault in red wine, unless very dominant, but it can make for a challenging flavour that might not appeal to all tastes.

liquorous – Wines of great weight and glyceriney texture (evidenced by the 'legs', or 'tears', which cling to the glass after the wine has been swirled) are always noteworthy. The connection with liquor is drawn in respect of the feel of the wine in the mouth, rather than with the higher alcoholic strength of spirits.

Lirac – Village and AC of southern Rhône Valley, France. A near-neighbour of the esteemed appellation of Châteauneuf du Pape, Lirac makes red wine of comparable depth and complexity, at competitive prices.

Lugana – DOC of Lombardy, Italy, known for a dry white wine that is often of real distinction – rich, almondy stuff from the ubiquitous Trebbiano grape.

M

Macabeo – One of the main grapes used for cava, the sparkling wine of Spain. It is the same grape as Viura.

Mâcon – Town and collective appellation of southern Burgundy, France. Minerally white wines from Chardonnay grapes and light reds from Pinot Noir and some Gamay. The better ones, and the ones exported, have the AC Mâcon-Villages and there are individual village wines with their own ACs including Mâcon-Clessé, Mâcon-Viré and Mâcon-Lugny.

Malbec – Black grape variety grown on a small scale in Bordeaux, and the mainstay of the wines of Cahors in France's Dordogne region under the name Cot. Now much better known for producing big butch reds in Argentina.

malolactic fermentation – In winemaking, a common natural bacterial action following alcoholic fermentation, converting malic (apple) acid into lactic (milk) acid. The effect is to reduce tartness and to boost creaminess in the wine. Adding lactic bacteria to wine to promote the process is widely practised.

manzanilla – Pale, very dry sherry of Sanlucar de Barrameda, a resort town on the Bay of Cadiz in Spain. Manzanilla is proud to be distinct from the pale, very dry fino sherry of the main producing town of Jerez de la Frontera an hour's drive inland. Drink it chilled and fresh – it goes downhill in an opened bottle after just a few days, even if kept (as it should be) in the fridge.

Margaret River – Vineyard region of Western Australia regarded as ideal for grape varieties including Cabernet Sauvignon. It has a relatively cool climate and a reputation for making sophisticated wines, both red and white.

Marlborough – Best-known vineyard region of New Zealand's South Island has a cool climate and a name for brisk but cerebral Sauvignon Blanc and Chardonnay wines.

Marsanne – White grape variety of the northern Rhône Valley and, increasingly, of the wider south of France. It's known for making well-coloured wines with heady aroma and nuanced fruit.

Mataro – Black grape variety of Australia. It's the same as the Mourvèdre of France and Monastrell of Spain.

Mazuelo – Spanish name for France's black grape variety Carignan.

McLaren Vale – Vineyard region south of Adelaide in south-east Australia. Known for blockbuster Shiraz (and Chardonnay) that can be of great balance and quality from winemakers who manage to keep the ripeness under control.

meaty – In wine-tasting, a weighty, rich red wine style.

Mencia – Black grape variety of Galicia and north-west Spain. Light red wines.

Mendoza – Wine region of Argentina. Lying to the east of the Andes mountains, just about opposite the best vineyards of Chile on the other side, Mendoza accounts for the bulk of Argentine wine production.

Merlot – One of the great black wine grapes of Bordeaux, and now grown all over the world. The name is said to derive from the French *merle*, a blackbird. Characteristics of Merlot-based wines attract descriptions such as 'plummy' and 'plump' with black-cherry aromas. The grapes are larger than most, and thus have less skin in proportion to their flesh. This means the resulting wines have less tannin than wines from smaller-berry varieties such as Cabernet Sauvignon, and are therefore, in the Bordeaux context at least, more suitable for drinking while still relatively young.

middle palate – In wine-tasting, the impression given by the wine after the first impact on 'entry' and before the 'finish' when the wine is swallowed.

Midi – Catch-all term for the deep south of France west of the Rhône Valley.

mineral – Irresistible term in wine-tasting. To me it evokes flavours such as the stone-pure freshness of some Loire dry whites, or the flinty quality of the more austere style of the Chardonnay grape, especially in Chablis. Mineral really just means something mined, as in dug out of the ground, like iron ore (as in 'steely' whites) or rock, as in, er, stone. Maybe there's something in it, but I am not entirely confident.

Minervois – AC for (mostly) red wines from vineyards around the Roman-founded town of Minerve in the Languedoc-Roussillon region of France. Often good value. The recently elevated Minervois La Livinière AC is a sort of Minervois *grand cru*.

Monastrell – Black grape variety of Spain, widely planted in Mediterranean regions for inexpensive wines notable for their high alcohol and toughness – though they can mature into excellent, soft reds. The variety is known in France as Mourvèdre and in Australia as Mataro.

Monbazillac – AC for sweet, dessert wines within the wider appellation of Bergerac in south-west France. Made from the same grape varieties (principally Sauvignon and Semillon) that go into the much costlier counterpart wines of Barsac and Sauternes near Bordeaux, these stickies from botrytis-affected, late-harvested grapes can be delicious and good value for money.

Montalcino – Hill town of Tuscany, Italy, and a DOCG for strong and very long-lived red wines from Brunello grapes. The wines are mostly very expensive. Rosso di Montalcino, a DOC for the humbler wines of the zone, is often a good buy.

Montepulciano – Black grape variety of Italy. Best known in Montepulciano d'Abruzzo, the juicy, purply-black and bramble-fruited red of the Abruzzi region midway down Italy's Adriatic side. Also the grape in the rightly popular hearty reds of Rosso Conero from around Ancona in the Marches. Not to be confused with the hill town of Montepulciano in Tuscany, famous for expensive Vino Nobile di Montepulciano wine, made from Sangiovese grapes.

morello – Lots of red wines have smells and flavours redolent of cherries. Morello cherries, among the darkest coloured and sweetest of all varieties and the preferred choice of cherry-brandy producers, have a distinct sweetness resembled by some wines made from Merlot grapes. A morello whiff or taste is generally very welcome.

Moscatel – Spanish Muscat.

Moscato – *See* Muscat.

moselle – The wine of Germany's Mosel river valleys, collectively known for winemaking purposes as the Mosel-Saar-Ruwer. The wine always comes in slim, green bottles, as distinct from the brown bottles traditionally, but no longer exclusively, employed for Rhine wines.

Mourvèdre – Widely planted black grape variety of southern France. It's an ingredient in many of the wines of Provence, the Rhône and Languedoc, including the ubiquitous Pays d'Oc. It's a hot-climate vine and the wine is usually blended with other varieties to give sweet aromas and 'backbone' to the mix. Known as Mataro in Australia and Monastrell in Spain.

Muscadet – One of France's most familiar everyday whites, made from a grape called the Melon or Melon de Bourgogne. It comes from vineyards at the estuarial end of the River Loire, and has a sea-breezy freshness about it. The better wines are reckoned to be those from the vineyards in the Sèvre et Maine region, and many are made *sur lie* – 'on the lees' – meaning that the wine is left in contact with the yeasty deposit of its fermentation until just before bottling, in an endeavour to add interest to what can sometimes be an acidic and fruitless style.

Muscat – Grape variety with origins in ancient Greece, and still grown widely among the Aegean islands for the production of sweet white wines. Muscats are the wines that taste more like grape juice than any other – but the high sugar levels ensure they are also among the most alcoholic of wines, too. Known as Moscato in Italy, the grape is much used for making sweet sparkling wines, as in Asti Spumante or Moscato d'Asti. There are several appellations in south-west France for inexpensive Muscats made rather like port, part-fermented before the addition of grape alcohol to halt the conversion of sugar into alcohol, creating a sweet and heady *vin doux naturel*. Dry Muscat wines, when well made, have a delicious sweet aroma but a refreshing, light touch with flavours reminiscent variously of orange blossom, wood smoke and grapefruit.

must – New-pressed grape juice prior to fermentation.

N

Navarra – DO wine-producing region of northern Spain adjacent to, and overshadowed by, Rioja. Navarra's wines can be startlingly akin to their neighbouring rivals, and sometimes rather better value for money.

négociant – In France, a dealer-producer who buys wines from growers and matures and/or blends them for bottling and sale under his or her own label. Purists can be a bit sniffy about these entrepreneurs, claiming that only the vine-grower with his or her own winemaking set-up can make truly authentic stuff, but the truth is that many of the best wines of France are *négociant*-produced – especially at the humbler end of the price scale. *Négociants* are often identified on wine labels as *négociant-éleveur* (literally 'dealer-bringer-up'), meaning that the wine has been matured, blended and bottled by the party in question.

Negroamaro – Black grape variety mainly of Puglia, the much-lauded wine region of south-east Italy. Dense, earthy red wines with ageing potential and plenty of alcohol. The name is probably (if not obviously) derived from Italian *negro* (black) and *amaro* (bitter). The grape behind Copertino, Salice Salentino and Squinzano.

Nerello Mascalese – Black grape of Sicily, most prolific in vineyards surrounding Mount Etna, making distinctive, flavoursome reds.

Nero d'Avola – Black grape variety of Sicily (Avola is a town in the province of Syracuse) and southern Italy. It makes deep-coloured wines that, given half a chance, can develop intensity and richness with age.

non-vintage – A wine is described as such when it has been blended from the harvests of more than one year. A non-vintage wine is not necessarily an inferior one, but under quality-control regulations around the world, still table wines most usually derive solely from one year's grape crop to qualify for appellation status. Champagnes and sparkling wines are mostly blended from several vintages, as are fortified wines such as port and sherry.

nose – In the vocabulary of the wine-taster, the nose is the scent of a wine. Sounds a bit dotty, but it makes a sensible enough alternative to the rather bald 'smell'. The use of the word 'perfume' implies that the wine smells particularly good. 'Aroma' is used specifically to describe a wine that smells as it should, as in 'this burgundy has the authentic strawberry-raspberry aroma of Pinot Noir'.

O

oak – Most of the world's costliest wines are matured in new or nearly new oak barrels, giving additional opulence of flavour. Of late, many cheaper wines have been getting the oak treatment, too, in older, cheaper casks, or simply by having sacks of oak chippings poured into their steel or fibreglass holding tanks. 'Oak aged' on a label is likely to indicate the latter treatments. But the overtly oaked wines of Australia have in some cases been so overdone that there is now a reactive trend whereby some producers proclaim their wines – particularly Chardonnays – as 'unoaked' on the label, thereby asserting that the flavours are more naturally achieved.

Oltrepo Pavese – Wine-producing zone of Piedmont, north-west Italy. The name means 'south of Pavia across the [river] Po' and the wines, both white and red, can be excellent quality and value for money.

organic wine – As in other sectors of the food industry, demand for organically made wine is – or appears to be – growing. As a rule, a wine qualifies as organic if it comes entirely from grapes grown in vineyards cultivated without the use of synthetic materials, and made in a winery where chemical treatments or additives are shunned with similar vigour. In fact, there are plenty of winemakers in the world using organic methods, but who disdain to label their bottles as such. Wines proclaiming their organic status used to carry the same sort of premium as their counterparts round the corner in the fruit, vegetable and meat aisles. But organic viticulture is now commonplace and there seems little price impact. There is no single worldwide (or even Europe-wide) standard for organic food or wine, so you pretty much have to take the producer's word for it.

P

Pasqua – One of the biggest and, it should be said, best wine producers of the Veneto region of north-west Italy.

Passerina – White grape variety of Marche, Italy. Used in blending but there is also a regional Passerina DOC.

Passetoutgrains – Designation for wine made from more than one grape variety grown in the same vineyard. French. Mostly red burgundy from Gamay and Pinot Noir.

Pays d'Oc – Shortened form under recent rule changes of French wine designation Vin de Pays d'Oc. All other similar regional designations can be similarly abbreviated.

Pecorino – White grape variety of mid-eastern Italy currently in vogue for well-coloured dry white varietal wines.

Periquita – Black grape variety of southern Portugal. Makes rather exotic spicy reds. Name means 'parrot'.

Perricone – Black grape variety of Sicily. Low-acid red wines.

PET – It's what they call plastic wine bottles – lighter to transport and allegedly as ecological as glass. Polyethylene terephthalate.

Petit Verdot – Black grape variety of Bordeaux contributing additional colour, density and spiciness to Cabernet Sauvignon-dominated blends. Mostly a minority player at home, but in Australia and California it is grown as the principal variety for some big hearty reds of real character.

petrol – When white wines from certain grapes, especially Riesling, are allowed to age in the bottle for longer than a year or two, they can take on a spirity aroma reminiscent of petrol or diesel. In grand mature German wines, this is considered a good thing.

Picpoul – Grape variety of southern France. Best known in Picpoul de Pinet, a dry white from near Sète on the Golfe de Lyon, lately elevated to AOP status. The name Picpoul (also Piquepoul) means 'stings the lips' – referring to the natural high acidity of the juice.

Piemonte – North-western province of Italy, which we call Piedmont, known for the spumante wines of the town of Asti, plus expensive Barbaresco and Barolo and better-value varietal red wines from Nebbiolo, Barbera and Dolcetto grapes.

Pinotage – South Africa's own black grape variety. Makes red wines ranging from light and juicy to dark, strong and long-lived. It's a cross between Pinot Noir and a grape the South Africans used to call Hermitage (thus the portmanteau name) but turns out to have been Cinsault.

Pinot Blanc – White grape variety principally of Alsace, France. Florally perfumed, exotically fruity dry white wines.

Pinot Grigio – White grape variety of northern Italy. Wines bearing its name are perplexingly fashionable. Good examples have an interesting smoky-pungent aroma and keen, slaking fruit. But most are dull. Originally French, it is at its best in the lushly exotic Pinot Gris wines of Alsace and is also successfully cultivated in Germany and New Zealand.

Pinot Noir – The great black grape of Burgundy, France. It makes all the region's fabulously expensive red wines. Notoriously difficult to grow in warmer climates, it is nevertheless cultivated by countless intrepid winemakers in the New World intent on reproducing the magic appeal of red burgundy. California and New Zealand have come closest. Some Chilean Pinot Noirs are inexpensive and worth trying.

Pouilly Fuissé – Village and AC of the Mâconnais region of southern Burgundy in France. Dry white wines from Chardonnay grapes. Wines are among the highest rated of the Mâconnais.

Pouilly Fumé – Village and AC of the Loire Valley in France. Dry white wines from Sauvignon Blanc grapes. Similar 'pebbly', 'grassy' or 'gooseberry' style to neighbouring AC Sancerre. The notion put about by some enthusiasts that Pouilly Fumé is 'smoky' is surely nothing more than word association with the name.

Primitivo – Black grape variety of southern Italy, especially the region of Puglia. Named from Latin *primus* for first, the grape is among the earliest-ripening of all varieties. The wines are typically dense and dark in colour with plenty of alcohol, and have an earthy, spicy style.

Priorat – Emerging wine region of Catalonia, Spain. Highly valued red wines from Garnacha and other varieties. Generic brands available in supermarkets are well worth trying out.

Prosecco – Softly sparkling wine of Italy's Veneto region. The best come from the DOCG Conegliano-Valdobbiadene, made as spumante ('foaming') wines in pressurised tanks, typically to 11 per cent alcohol and ranging from softly sweet to crisply dry. The constituent grape, previously also known as Prosecco, has been officially assigned the name Glera.

Puglia – The region occupying the 'heel' of southern Italy, making many good, inexpensive wines from indigenous grape varieties.

Q

QbA – German, standing for Qualitätswein bestimmter Anbaugebiete. It means 'quality wine from designated areas' and implies that the wine is made from grapes with a minimum level of ripeness, but it's by no means a guarantee of exciting quality. Only wines labelled QmP (see next entry) can be depended upon to be special.

QmP – Stands for Qualitätswein mit Prädikat. These are the serious wines of Germany, made without the addition of sugar to 'improve' them. To qualify for QmP status, the grapes must reach a level of ripeness as measured on a sweetness scale – all according to Germany's fiendishly complicated wine-quality regulations. Wines from grapes that reach the stated minimum level of sweetness qualify for the description of Kabinett. The next level up earns the rank of Spätlese, meaning 'late-picked'. Kabinett wines can be expected to be dry and brisk in style, and Spätlese wines a little bit riper and fuller. The next grade up, Auslese, meaning 'selected harvest', indicates a wine made from super-ripe grapes; it will be golden in colour and honeyed in flavour. A generation ago, these wines were as valued, and as expensive, as any of the world's grandest appellations. Beerenauslese and Trockenbeerenauslese are speciality wines made from individually picked late-harvest grapes.

Quincy – AC of Loire Valley, France, known for pebbly-dry white wines from Sauvignon grapes. The wines are forever compared to those of nearby and much better-known Sancerre – and Quincy often represents better value for money. Pronounced 'KAN-see'.

Quinta – Portuguese for farm or estate. It precedes the names of many of Portugal's best-known wines. It is pronounced 'KEEN-ta'.

R

racy – Evocative wine-tasting description for wine that thrills the tastebuds with a rush of exciting sensations. Good Rieslings often qualify.

raisiny – Wines from grapes that have been very ripe or overripe at harvest can take on a smell and flavour akin to the concentrated, heat-dried sweetness of raisins. As a minor element in the character of a wine, this can add to the appeal but as a dominant characteristic it is a fault.

rancio – Spanish term harking back to Roman times when wines were commonly stored in jars outside, exposed to the sun, so they oxidised and took on a burnt sort of flavour. Today, *rancio* describes a baked – and by no means unpleasant – flavour in fortified wines, particularly sherry and Madeira.

Reserva – In Portugal and Spain, this has genuine significance. The Portuguese use it for special wines with a higher alcohol level and longer ageing, although the precise periods vary between regions. In Spain, especially in the Navarra and Rioja regions, it means the wine must have had at least a year in oak and two in bottle before release.

reserve – On French (as *réserve*) or other wines, this implies special-quality, longer-aged wines, but has no official significance.

residual sugar – There is sugar in all wine, left over from the fermentation process. Some producers now mention the quantity of residual sugar on back labels in grams per litre of wine, even though so far there is no legal obligation to do so. Dry wines, red or white, typically have 3 g/l or fewer. Above that, you might well be able to taste the sweetness. In southern hemisphere wines, made from grapes that have ripened under more-intense sunlight than their European counterparts, sugar levels can be correspondingly higher. Sweet wines such as Sauternes contain up to 150 g/l. Dry ('brut') sparkling wines made by the 'champagne' method typically have 10 g/l and tank-method fizzes such as prosecco up to 15 g/l.

Retsina – The universal white wine of Greece. It has been traditionally made in Attica, the region of Athens, for a very long time, and is said to owe its origins and name to the ancient custom of sealing amphorae (terracotta jars) of the wine with a gum made from pine resin. Some of the flavour of the resin inevitably transmitted itself into the wine, and ancient Greeks acquired a lasting taste for it.

Reuilly – AC of Loire Valley, France, for crisp dry whites from Sauvignon grapes. Pronounced 'RER-yee'.

Ribatejo – Emerging wine region of Portugal. Worth seeking out on labels of red wines in particular, because new winemakers are producing lively stuff from distinctive indigenous grapes such as Castelao and Trincadeira.

Ribera del Duero – Classic wine region of north-west Spain lying along the River Duero (which crosses the border to become Portugal's Douro, forming the valley where port comes from). It is home to an estate oddly named Vega Sicilia, where red wines of epic quality are made and sold at equally epic prices. Further down the scale, some very good reds are made, too.

Riesling – The noble grape variety of Germany. It is correctly pronounced 'REEZ-ling', not 'RICE-ling'. Once notorious as the grape behind all those boring 'medium' Liebfraumilches and Niersteiners, this grape has had a bad press. In fact, there has never been much, if any, Riesling in German plonk. But the country's best wines, the so-called Qualitätswein mit Prädikat grades, are made almost exclusively with Riesling. These wines range from crisply fresh and appley styles to extravagantly fruity, honeyed wines from late-harvested grapes. Excellent Riesling wines are also made in Alsace and now in Australasia.

Rioja – The principal fine-wine region of Spain, in the country's north east. The pricier wines are noted for their vanilla-pod richness from long ageing in oak casks. Tempranillo and Garnacha grapes make the reds, Viura the whites.

Ripasso – A particular style of Valpolicella wine. New wine is partially refermented in vats that have been used to make Recioto reds (wines made from semi-dried grapes), thus creating a bigger, smoother version of usually light and pale Valpolicella.

Riserva – In Italy, a wine made only in the best vintages, and allowed longer ageing in cask and bottle.

Rivaner – Alternative name for Germany's Müller-Thurgau grape.

Riverland – Vineyard region to the immediate north of the Barossa Valley of South Australia, extending east into New South Wales.

Roditis – White grape variety of Greece, known for fresh dry whites with decent acidity, often included in retsina.

rosso – Red wine, Italy.

Rosso Conero – DOC red wine made in the environs of Ancona in the Marches, Italy. Made from the Montepulciano grape, the wine can provide excellent value for money.

Ruby Cabernet – Black grape variety of California, created by crossing Cabernet Sauvignon and Carignan. Makes soft and squelchy red wine at home and in South Africa.

Rueda – DO of north-west Spain making first-class refreshing dry whites from the indigenous Verdejo grape, imported Sauvignon, and others. Exciting quality, and prices are keen.

Rully – AC of Chalonnais region of southern Burgundy, France. White wines from Chardonnay and red wines from Pinot Noir grapes. Both can be very good and substantially cheaper than their more northerly Burgundian neighbours. Pronounced 'ROO-yee'.

S

Sagrantino – Black grape variety native to Perugia, Italy. Dark, tannic wines best known in DOCG Sagrantino de Montefalco. Now also cultivated in Australia.

Saint Emilion – AC of Bordeaux, France. Centred on the romantic hill town of St Emilion, this famous sub-region makes some of the grandest red wines of France, but also some of the best-value ones. Less fashionable than the Médoc region on the opposite (west) bank of the River Gironde that bisects Bordeaux, St Emilion wines are made largely with the Merlot grape, and are relatively quick to mature. The top wines are classified *1er grand cru classé* and are madly expensive, but many more are classified respectively *grand cru classé* and *grand cru*, and these designations can be seen as a fairly trustworthy indicator of quality. There are several 'satellite' St Emilion ACs named after the villages at their centres, notably Lussac St Emilion, Montagne St Emilion and Puisseguin St Emilion. Some excellent wines are made by estates within these ACs, and at relatively affordable prices thanks to the comparatively humble status of their satellite designations.

Salento – Up-and-coming wine region of southern Italy. Many good bargain reds from local grapes including Nero d'Avola and Primitivo.

Sancerre – AC of the Loire Valley, France, renowned for flinty-fresh Sauvignon Blanc whites and rarer Pinot Noir reds and rosés.

Sangiovese – The local black grape of Tuscany, Italy, is the principal variety used for Chianti. Also planted further south in Italy and in the

New World. Generic Sangiovese di Toscana can make a consoling substitute for costly Chianti.

Saumur – Town and appellation of Loire Valley, France. Characterful minerally red wines from Cabernet Franc grapes, and some whites. Sparkling wines from Chenin Blanc grapes can be good value.

Saumur-Champigny – Separate appellation for red wines from Cabernet Franc grapes of Saumur in the Loire, sometimes very good and lively.

Sauvignon Blanc – French white grape variety now grown worldwide. New Zealand has raised worldwide production values challenging the long supremacy of French ACs in Bordeaux and the Loire Valley. Chile and South Africa aspire similarly. The wines are characterised by aromas of gooseberry, peapod, fresh-cut grass, even asparagus. Flavours are often described as 'grassy' or 'nettly'.

sec – Dry wine style. French.

secco – Dry wine style. Italian.

seco – Dry wine style. Spanish.

Semillon – White grape variety originally of Bordeaux, where it is blended with Sauvignon Blanc to make fresh dry whites and, when harvested very late in the season, the ambrosial sweet whites of Barsac, Sauternes and other appellations. Even in the driest wines, the grape can be recognised from its honeyed, sweet-pineapple, even banana-like aromas. Now widely planted in Australia and Latin America, and frequently blended with Chardonnay to make dry whites, some of them interesting.

sherry – The great aperitif wine of Spain, centred on the Andalusian city of Jerez (the name 'sherry' is an English mispronunciation). There is a lot of sherry-style wine in the world, but only the authentic wine from Jerez and the neighbouring producing centres of Puerta de Santa Maria and Sanlucar de Barrameda may label their wines as such. The Spanish drink real sherry – very dry and fresh, pale in colour and served well-chilled – called fino and manzanilla, and darker but naturally dry variations called amontillado, palo cortado and oloroso.

Shiraz – Australian name for the Syrah grape. The variety is the most widely planted of any in Australia, and makes red wines of wildly varying quality, characterised by dense colour, high alcohol, spicy fruit and generous, cushiony texture.

Somontano – Wine region of north-east Spain. Name means 'under the mountains' – in this case the Pyrenees – and the region has had DO status since 1984. Much innovative winemaking here, with New World styles emerging. Some very good buys. A region to watch.

souple – French wine-tasting term that translates into English as 'supple' or even 'docile' as in 'pliable', but I understand it in the vinous context to mean muscular but soft – a wine with tannin as well as soft fruit.

Spätlese – *See* QmP.

spirity – Some wines, mostly from the New World, are made from grapes so ripe at harvest that their high alcohol content can be detected through a mildly burning sensation on the tongue, similar to the effect of sipping a spirit. Young Port wines can be detectably spirity.

spritzy – Describes a wine with a gentle sparkle. Some young wines are intended to have this elusive fizziness; in others it is a fault.

spumante – Sparkling wine of Italy. Asti Spumante is the best known, from the town of Asti in the north-west Italian province of Piemonte. Many Prosecco wines are labelled as Spumante in style. The term describes wines that are fully sparkling. Frizzante wines have a less vigorous mousse.

stalky – A useful tasting term to describe red wines with flavours that make you think the stalks from the grape bunches must have been fermented along with the must (juice). Red Loire wines and youthful claret very often have this mild astringency. In moderation it's fine, but if it dominates it probably signifies the wine is at best immature and at worst badly made.

Stellenbosch – Town and region at the heart of South Africa's wine industry. It's an hour's drive from Cape Town and the source of much of the country's cheaper wine. Some serious-quality estate wines as well.

stony – Wine-tasting term for keenly dry white wines. It's meant to indicate a wine of purity and real quality, with just the right match of fruit and acidity.

structured – Good wines are not one-dimensional, they have layers of flavour and texture. A structured wine has phases of enjoyment: the 'attack', or first impression in the mouth; the middle palate as the wine is held in the mouth; and the lingering aftertaste.

sugar – *See* residual sugar.

sulphites – Nearly all wines, barring some esoteric 'natural' types of a kind not found in supermarkets are made with the aid of preparations containing sulphur to combat diseases in the vineyards and bacterial infections in the winery. It's difficult to make wine without sulphur. Even 'organic' wines need it. Because some people are sensitive to the traces of sulphur in some wines, worldwide health authorities insist wine labels bear the warning 'Contains sulphites'.

summer fruit – Wine-tasting term intended to convey a smell or taste of soft fruits such as strawberries and raspberries – without having to commit too specifically to which.

superiore – On labels of Italian wines, this is more than an idle boast. Under DOC(G) rules, wines must qualify for the *superiore* designation by reaching one or more specified quality levels, usually a higher alcohol content or an additional period of maturation. Frascati, for example, qualifies for DOC status at 11.5 per cent alcohol, but to be classified *superiore* must have 12 per cent alcohol.

sur lie – Literally, 'on the lees'. It's a term now widely used on the labels of Muscadet wines, signifying that after fermentation has died down, the new wine has been left in the tank over the winter on the lees – the detritus of yeasts and other interesting compounds left over from the turbid fermentation process. The idea is that additional interest is imparted into the flavour of the wine.

Syrah – The noble grape of the Rhône Valley, France. Makes very dark, dense wine characterised by peppery, tarry aromas. Now planted all over southern France and farther afield. In Australia it is known as Shiraz.

T

table wine – Wine that is unfortified and of an alcoholic strength, for UK tax purposes anyway, of no more than 15 per cent. I use the term to distinguish, for example, between the red table wines of the Douro Valley in Portugal and the region's better-known fortified wine, port.

Tafelwein – Table wine, German. The humblest quality designation, which doesn't usually bode very well.

tank method – Bulk-production process for sparkling wines. Base wine undergoes secondary fermentation in a large, sealed vat rather than in individual closed bottles. Also known as the Charmat method after the name of the inventor of the process. Prosecco is made by the tank method.

Tai – White grape variety of north-east Italy, a relative of Sauvignon Blanc. Also known in Italy as Tocai Friulano or, more correctly, Friulano.

Tannat – Black grape of south-west France, notably for wines of Madiran, and lately named as the variety most beneficial to health thanks to its outstanding antioxidant content.

tannin – Well known as the film-forming, teeth-coating component in tea, tannin is a natural compound that occurs in black grape skins and acts as a natural preservative in wine. Its noticeable presence in wine is regarded as a good thing. It gives young everyday reds their dryness, firmness of flavour and backbone. And it helps high-quality reds to retain their lively fruitiness for many years. A grand Bordeaux red when first made, for example, will have purply-sweet, rich fruit and mouth-puckering tannin, but after ten years or so this will have evolved into a delectably fruity, mature wine in which the formerly parching effects of the tannin have receded almost completely, leaving the shade of 'residual tannin' that marks out a great wine approaching maturity.

Tarrango – Black grape variety of Australia.

tarry – On the whole, winemakers don't like critics to say their wines evoke the redolence of road repairs, but I can't help using this term to describe the agreeable, sweet, 'burnt' flavour that is often found at the centre of the fruit in red wines from Argentina, Italy, Portugal and South Africa in particular.

TCA – Dreaded ailment in wine, usually blamed on faulty corks. It stands for 246 *trichloroanisol* and is characterised by a horrible musty smell and flavour in the affected wine. Thanks to technological advances made by cork manufacturers in Portugal – the leading cork nation – TCA is now in retreat.

tears – The colourless alcohol in the wine left clinging to the inside of the glass after the contents have been swirled. Persistent tears (also known as 'legs') indicate a wine of good concentration.

Tempranillo – The great black grape of Spain. Along with Garnacha (Grenache in France) it makes most red Rioja and Navarra wines and, under many pseudonyms, is an important or exclusive contributor to the wines of many other regions of Spain. It is also widely cultivated in South America.

Teroldego – Black grape variety of Trentino, northern Italy. Often known as Teroldego Rotaliano after the Rotaliano region where most of the vineyards lie. Deep-coloured, assertive, green-edged red wines.

terroir – French word for 'ground' or 'soil' has mystical meaning in vineyard country. Winemakers attribute the distinct characteristics of their products, not just to the soil conditions but to the lie of the land and the prevailing (micro)climate, all within the realm of terroir. The word now frequently appears on effusive back labels asserting the unique appeal of the wine. Some critics scoff that terroir is all imagined nonsense.

tinto – On Spanish labels indicates a deeply coloured red wine. Clarete denotes a paler colour. Also Portuguese.

Toro – Quality wine region east of Zamora, Spain.

Torrontes – White grape variety of Argentina. Makes soft, dry wines often with delicious grapey-spicy aroma, similar in style to the classic dry Muscat wines of Alsace, but at more accessible prices.

Touraine – Region encompassing a swathe of the Loire Valley, France. Non-AC wines may be labelled 'Sauvignon de Touraine'.

Touriga Nacional – The most valued black grape variety of the Douro Valley in Portugal, where port is made. The name Touriga now appears on an increasing number of table wines made as sidelines by the port producers. They can be very good, with the same spirity aroma and sleek flavours of port itself, minus the fortification.

Traminer – Grape variety, the same as Gewürztraminer.

Trebbiano – The workhorse white grape of Italy. A productive variety that is easy to cultivate, it seems to be included in just about every ordinary white wine of the entire nation – including Frascati, Orvieto and Soave. It is the same grape as France's Ugni Blanc. There are, however, distinct regional variations of the grape. Trebbiano di Lugana (also known as Turbiana) makes a distinctive white in the DOC of the name, sometimes very good, while Trebbiano di Toscana makes a major contribution to the distinctly less interesting dry whites of Chianti country.

Trincadeira Preta – Portuguese black grape variety native to the port-producing vineyards of the Douro Valley (where it goes under the name Tinta Amarella). In southern Portugal, it produces dark and sturdy table wines.

trocken – 'Dry' German wine. The description does have a particular meaning under German wine law, namely that there is only a low level of unfermented sugar lingering in the wine (9 grams per litre, if you need to know), and this can leave the wine tasting rather austere.

U

Ugni Blanc – The most widely cultivated white grape variety of France and the mainstay of many a cheap dry white wine. To date it has been better known as the provider of base wine for distilling into armagnac and cognac, but lately the name has been appearing on wine labels. Technology seems to be improving the performance of the grape. The curious name is pronounced 'OON-yee', and is the same variety as Italy's ubiquitous Trebbiano.

Utiel-Requena – Region and *Denominación de Origen* of Mediterranean Spain inland from Valencia. Principally red wines from Bobal, Garnacha and Tempranillo grapes grown at relatively high altitude, between 600 and 900 metres.

V

Vacqueyras – Village of the southern Rhône Valley of France in the region better known for its generic appellation, the Côtes du Rhône.

Vacqueyras can date its winemaking history all the way back to 1414, but has only been producing under its own village AC since 1991. The wines, from Grenache and Syrah grapes, can be wonderfully silky and intense, spicy and long-lived.

Valdepeñas – An island of quality production amidst the ocean of mediocrity that is Spain's La Mancha region – where most of the grapes are grown for distilling into the head-banging brandies of Jerez. Valdepeñas reds are made from a grape they call the Cencibel – which turns out to be a very close relation of the Tempranillo grape that is the mainstay of the fine but expensive red wines of Rioja. Again, like Rioja, Valdepeñas wines are matured in oak casks to give them a vanilla-rich smoothness. Among bargain reds, Valdepeñas is a name to look out for.

Valpolicella – Red wine of Verona, Italy. Good examples have ripe, cherry fruit and a pleasingly dry finish. Unfortunately, there are many bad examples of Valpolicella. Shop with circumspection. Valpolicella Classico wines, from the best vineyards clustered around the town, are more reliable. Those additionally labelled *superiore* have higher alcohol and some bottle age.

vanilla – Ageing wines in oak barrels (or, less picturesquely, adding oak chips to wine in huge concrete vats) imparts a range of characteristics including a smell of vanilla from the ethyl vanilline naturally given off by oak.

varietal – A varietal wine is one named after the grape variety (one or more) from which it is made. Nearly all everyday wines worldwide are now labelled in this way. It is salutary to contemplate that until the present wine boom began in the 1980s, wines described thus were virtually unknown outside Germany and one or two quirky regions of France and Italy.

vegan-friendly – My informal way of noting that a wine is claimed to have been made not only with animal-product-free finings (*see* vegetarian wine) but without any animal-related products whatsoever, such as livestock manure in the vineyards.

vegetal – A tasting note definitely open to interpretation. It suggests a smell or flavour reminiscent less of fruit (apple, pineapple, strawberry and the like) than of something leafy or even root based. Some wines are evocative (to some tastes) of beetroot, cabbage or even unlikelier vegetable flavours – and these characteristics may add materially to the attraction of the wine.

vegetarian wine – Wines labelled 'suitable for vegetarians' have been made without the assistance of animal products for 'fining' – clarifying – before bottling. Gelatine, egg whites, isinglass from fish bladders and casein from milk are among the items shunned, usually in favour of bentonite, an absorbent clay first found at Benton in the US state of Montana.

Verdejo – White grape of the Rueda region in north-west Spain. It can make superbly perfumed crisp dry whites of truly distinctive character and has helped make Rueda one of the best white-wine sources of Europe. No relation to Verdelho.

Verdelho – Portuguese grape variety once mainly used for a medium-dry style of Madeira, also called Verdelho, but now rare. The vine is now prospering in Australia, where it can make well-balanced dry whites with fleeting richness and lemon-lime acidity.

Verdicchio – White grape variety of Italy best known in the DOC zone of Castelli di Jesi in the Adriatic wine region of the Marches. Dry white wines once known for little more than their naff amphora-style bottles but now gaining a reputation for interesting, herbaceous flavours of recognisable character.

Vermentino – White grape variety principally of Italy, especially Sardinia. Makes florally scented soft dry whites.

Vieilles vignes – Old vines. Many French producers like to claim on their labels that the wine within is from vines of notable antiquity. While it's true that vines don't produce useful grapes for the first few years after planting, it is uncertain whether vines of much greater age – say 25 years plus – than others actually make better fruit. There are no regulations governing the use of the term, so it's not a reliable indicator anyway.

Vin de France – In effect, the new Vin de Table of France's morphing wine laws. The label may state the vintage (if all the wine in the blend does come from a single year's harvest) and the grape varieties that constitute the wine. It may not state the region of France from which the wine originates.

vin de liqueur – Sweet style of white wine mostly from the Pyrenean region of south-westernmost France, made by adding a little spirit to the new wine before it has fermented out, halting the fermentation and retaining sugar.

vin de pays – 'Country wine' of France. Introduced in 1968 and regularly revised ever since, it's the wine-quality designation between basic Vin de France and AOC/AOP. Although being superseded by the more recently introduced IGP (*qv*), there are more than 150 producing areas permitted to use the description vin de pays. Some vin de pays areas are huge: the Vin de Pays d'Oc (referencing the Languedoc region) covers much of the Midi and Provence. Plenty of wines bearing this humble designation are of astoundingly high quality and certainly compete with New World counterparts for interest and value. *See* Indication Géographique Protégée.

vin de table – Formerly official designation of generic French wine, now used only informally. *See* Vin de France.

vin doux naturel – Sweet, mildly fortified wine of southern France. A little spirit is added during the winemaking process, halting the fermentation by killing the yeast before it has consumed all the sugars – hence the pronounced sweetness of the wine.

vin gris – Rosé wine from Provence.

Vinho de mesa – 'Table wine' of Portugal.

Vino da tavola – The humblest official classification of Italian wine. Much ordinary plonk bears this designation, but the bizarre quirks of Italy's wine laws dictate that some of that country's finest wines are also classed as mere vino da tavola (table wine). If an expensive Italian wine is labelled as such, it doesn't mean it will be a disappointment.

Vino de la Tierra – Generic classification for regional wines, Spain. Abbreviates to VdT.

Vino de mesa – 'Table wine' of Spain. Usually very ordinary.

vintage – The grape harvest. The year displayed on bottle labels is the year of the harvest. Wines bearing no date have been blended from the harvests of two or more years.

Viognier – A white grape variety once exclusive to the northern Rhône Valley in France where it makes expensive Condrieu. Now, Viognier is grown more widely, in North and South America as well as elsewhere in France, and occasionally produces soft, marrowy whites that echo the grand style of Condrieu itself. The Viognier is now commonly blended with Shiraz in red winemaking in Australia and South Africa. It does not dilute the colour and is confidently believed by highly experienced winemakers to enhance the quality. Steve Webber, in charge of winemaking at the revered De Bortoli estates in the Yarra Valley region of Victoria, Australia, puts between two and five per cent Viognier in with some of his Shiraz wines. 'I think it's the perfume,' he told me. 'It gives some femininity to the wine.'

Viura – White grape variety of Rioja, Spain. Also widely grown elsewhere in Spain under the name Macabeo. Wines have a blossomy aroma and are dry, but sometimes soft at the expense of acidity.

Vouvray – AC of the Loire Valley, France, known for still and sparkling dry white wines and sweet, still whites from late-harvested grapes. The wines, all from Chenin Blanc grapes, have a unique capacity for unctuous softness combined with lively freshness – an effect best portrayed in the demi-sec (slightly sweet) wines, which can be delicious and keenly priced.

Vranac – Black grape variety of the Balkans known for dense colour and tangy-bitter edge to the flavour. Best enjoyed in situ.

W

weight – In an ideal world the weight of a wine is determined by the ripeness of the grapes from which it has been made. In some cases the weight is determined merely by the quantity of sugar added during the production process. A good, genuine wine described as having weight is one in which there is plenty of alcohol and 'extract' – colour and flavour from the grapes. Wine enthusiasts judge weight by swirling the wine in the glass and then examining the 'legs' or 'tears' left clinging to the inside of the glass after the contents have subsided. Alcohol gives these runlets a dense, glycerine-like condition, and if they cling for a long time, the wine is deemed to have weight – a very good thing in all honestly made wines.

Winzergenossenschaft – One of the many very lengthy and peculiar words regularly found on labels of German wines. This means a winemaking co- operative. Many excellent German wines are made by these associations of growers.

woody – A subjective tasting note. A faintly rank odour or flavour suggesting the wine has spent too long in cask.

X

Xarel-lo – One of the main grape varieties for cava, the sparkling wine of Spain.

Xinomavro – Black grape variety of Greece. It retains its acidity even in the very hot conditions that prevail in many Greek vineyards, where harvests tend to over-ripen and make cooked-tasting wines. Modern winemaking techniques are capable of making well-balanced wines from Xinomavro.

Y

Yecla – Town and DO wine region of eastern Spain, close to Alicante, making interesting, strong-flavoured red and white wines, often at bargain prices.

yellow – White wines are not white at all, but various shades of yellow – or, more poetically, gold. Some white wines with opulent richness even have a flavour I cannot resist calling yellow – reminiscent of butter.

Z

Zibibbo – Sicilian white grape variety synonymous with north African variety Muscat of Alexandria. Scantily employed in sweet winemaking, and occasionally for drier styles.

Zierfandler – Esoteric white grape of Thermenregion, Austria. Aromatic dry wines and rare late-harvest sweet wines.

Zinfandel – Black grape variety of California. Makes brambly reds, some of which can age very gracefully, and 'blush' whites – actually pink, because a little of the skin colour is allowed to leach into the must. The vine is also planted in Australia and South America. The Primitivo of southern Italy is said to be a related variety, but makes a very different kind of wine.

Zweigelt – Black grape of Austria making juicy red wines for drinking young. Some wines are aged in oak to make interesting, heftier long-keepers.

Index